The Immigrants

by
Charles Victor Palmer

Cover photo by Edwin Levick,
Courtesy Library of Congress

Copyright © 1997
by Charles Victor Palmer

4433 N.W. 47th Street
Oklahoma City, OK 73112

ISBN 1-886698-08-2

Library of Congress Catalog Card Number:
96-70981

FOREWORD

The following pages record events in the lives of what might be described as a middle class American family, the Palmers. No attempt has been made to change or dramatize their story.

The first part consists of events related to the author by relatives and friends. Subsequent happenings are taken from his own experience and observation. This book is largely autobiographical. Comments and views expressed are solely the opinions of the author. Hopefully, future generations will find it worth the reading, if only to get a glimpse of our lives and the way the world was in our time.

CVP

Contents

BOOK I

CHAPTER I

Sweden

In the year of 1877 on a farm near Ljungby, Sweden, in the province of Smaland, a child was born to Frederick and Sara Palm.

Frederick had been a sailor in the Swedish king's navy. In accordance with custom promoted vigorously at the time, he had changed his name. Since ancient times Scandinavians had named their children by adding "son" to the father's first name to produce the child's last name. Frederick decided to put an end to this custom in his family, so his first born son was named Andrew Palm.

The second son, born two years later in 1879, was named Charles Frederick, followed by Jonas Walfred in 1881, Axel born in 1885, Werner in 1886, and Anna in 1893. The children all survived to maturity, which considering the high infant mortality rate of the times, was unusual.

Fredrick was a slow easygoing individual, tall, thin and with the popular long handlebar mustache. Sarah, his wife, was dark haired, blue eyed, and with a straight but not prominent nose. Photographs of the time indicate that she was a beautiful woman of about five feet and four inches, her face bearing the stamp of good, forth-right character.

Tending the farm and cattle provided the family's basic needs as the children grew from childhood into their teens. Swedish land was not very fertile, and almost all of it was under cultivation, except the mountainous region where the forests grew. There was no room to grow. A change from farming into the trades meant little in the way of a more gainful occupation.

As the children grew older and began to think of their futures in Sweden, they seemed to encounter an insurmountable blank wall.

But there was America. Accounts circulated, of neighbors who had emigrated to the United States, stories of their success in the new land. But Frederick seemed rooted to his small patch of land in Smaland. Destiny and livelihood for the future fell squarely onto the laps of the young. Like birds barely able to fly, one by one the older ones began their precarious departure from the nest.

Andrew, the oldest, took off for Chicago where a distant relative "uncle" Andy Anderson lived. Andy was a boilermaker for the Standard Oil Company. The tailor's trade appealed to Andrew, and he was soon engaged as an apprentice at a tailor shop. It would be difficult to underestimate the effect of Andrew's emigration and his success in finding work upon the younger Palms. To follow in his path across the ocean rose to first place in their ambitions.

Charlie had weighed two and one-half pounds at birth. But in time he grew to average height. Farm work had developed his muscles so that he was strong for his size. Who can say whether it was heredity or the hard bread, or both, that gave him a perfect set of teeth that gleamed when he laughed or smiled?

There was a pear tree near the Palm's farmhouse, and when the fruit was ripe, he would shake the tree and the pears would come. There was little fruit grown in Sweden at the time, so this harvest left an indelible impression on his mind.

When the barn chores were finished, he and his brother Axel hoed weeds in the potato or sugar beet fields. The neighbors hired them for a few days to help on nearby farms.

At the age of sixteen, Charlie decided that he was old enough to emigrate to the United States. He too, turned up at "uncle " Andy's in Chicago. Andrew, now settled in his apprenticeship, had moved into quarters of his own. How Charlie got the money for his fare on the boat and for food remains unknown. Presumably, he earned a part of it in Sweden, or was given some, or borrowed some from Andrew. He never spoke of such matters to his children in later years, and in those days it would have been presumptuous of them to ask. He was soon employed at odd jobs, earning enough to liquidate debts if any and saving for his first plunge into a career of his own.

It was in Chicago that, out of curiosity, he happened to step into a dance hall to see what was going on. He watched the couples twirling about in the dances fashionable at the time and decided that he just had to learn to dance. There was a dancing school nearby, so he enrolled. In order to graduate, it was necessary to waltz smoothly enough so that a wine glass balanced on the head would not fall off. He was a very proud young man when he received his diploma. It was the first success that he tasted in the states.

They were all seated at the table for Thanksgiving dinner the next fall, when the dining room door was opened from the outside, and they looked up to see who had entered. A stranger stepped in, pulled a pistol from his coat pocket, and ordered everyone to remain seated. He then proceeded around the table, stopping to relieve each one of his money or valuable items. As he went around the table, Charlie noticed Uncle Andy, white as a sheet, starting to ladle some gravy onto his potatoes. The robber approached and searched him, taking his wallet. As the thug turned to the next victim, Andy shoved the bowl of hot gravy full in his face. It is assumed that the robber was subdued, as the story ended at that point.

Newspapers of the time carried stories of iron ore discoveries and development, in northern Minnesota on the Mesaba range. The few years that Charlie lived in Chicago convinced him that the hustle and bustle of a big city was not for him. As soon as he was financially able, he purchased a railway ticket and headed for Duluth, then transferred to the newly built railroad bound for Virginia, Minnesota.

The railway coaches in which he traveled and the land through which he journeyed are of passing interest. There were wicker, or red plush seats in the coaches. Light was provided at night by means of frosted globe kerosene lamps, and for heat, each coach had a pot bellied coal stove. There were no sleeping accommodations.

Soon after leaving Chicago the farms and truck gardens thinned out and then disappeared, to be replaced by a forest wilderness. Stops were made at small villages for passengers, and occasionally at sidings to drop lumberjacks off the train with their backpacks. The trip must have been slow and tedious. But Charlie liked to visit with people, and in all probability he enjoyed much of the journey. Perhaps the conversation was concerned with the passing scene and of prospects at the end of the line. It was not the custom to talk of thoughts or feelings with other people. If Charlie faced the future with concern or a measure of nervousness, it will never be known.

Nearing Duluth, the great forests of Wisconsin were broken occasionally by glimpses of a vast expanse of water to the north as the train approached Lake Superior. After a brief stop at Superior, Wisconsin, to let passengers off, the train moved slowly toward the bay, turning to cross the water on a bridge. The engine turned to the right and picked its way carefully through a maze of tracks. Drivers idling, it eased into the station. The brakes took hold and it stopped, panting slowly as if exhausted.

The passengers, tired and stiff, but spurred on by the need to collect their baggage and leave, hurried about the coach. Charlie stepped down to the plank platform with his two straw suitcases and looked about for a place to get breakfast. There was a restaurant across the street. While eating, he was surprised to hear many of the diners speaking the Swedish language, or talking English with a Swedish accent. It was reassuring to find so many "old country" people already settled and busily at work on their various jobs.

Back at the depot, he boarded a smaller passenger train. The engine with its baggage car and two coaches ran for some distance parallel to the bay, then swung westward through a divide, past the railway repair shops of Proctor and into a new wilderness. Now there were no villages. Forests alternated with swamps along the way, punctuated at intervals by sidings stacked with logs. It was

4

almost noon when the scene slipping past Charlie's window began to change. A range of small hills came into view. Scattered shacks and houses appeared upon the cleared land. The locomotive labored its way heavily around a large hill and began to coast. As the conductor announced, "Virginia next stop," Charlie collected his suitcases. He stepped from the coach onto the platform and into the first scenes of his adult career.

The Svea Hotel was owned by the Carlsons. Charlie spied the Swedish name while walking eastward from the train depot. He quickly rented a room above the dining hall and carried his bags up the stairs. The long journey had made him weary, and he laid down on the bed. Later, a knock on the door awakened him. It was supper time and he realized that he had slept for six hours. Hastily he washed his face, combed his hair, and descended to the dining room. Meals were served family style at a large boarding house table. The food was carried in large bowls or platters from the kitchen by the female help.

Around the table sat workers of all descriptions, their faces hastily scrubbed to remove the day's grime. Learning that Charlie was new in town and looking for work, they offered several suggestions for job opportunities. Meanwhile he made the acquaintance of Mrs. Carlson, the proprietress, who came to the table to meet her new boarder. She was not shy about asking questions, and soon everyone at the table had a brief history of his travels from Sweden and of his former life there.

Finding a job concerned Charlie the most. But he found that it was amazingly easy. Mining operations were expanding and men were in short supply. One could even choose among various occupations that needed operators. Charlie became a mechanic, ministering to the ore cars and the little saddle back locomotives that pushed loads of iron ore up from the newly dug pits. So at the age of nineteen, unskilled , with but a start in the mastery of the English Language, a callow youth in appearance, he began his metamorphosis toward becoming a mature American.

This story is interrupted to return in time and place to another European country, Finland, and to the year 1881.

CHAPTER II

Finland

Finland in the year 1881 was an arch duchy under the Czar of Russia. Contrary to conditions in Russia proper, the farmers were not slaves of the nobility. But few Finns owned the land they tilled. Rich landowners had gained possession of the arable land, and it was divided up into farms which families of tenants cultivated generation after generation. Seldom was a tenant evicted from his tract. He paid his rent by giving the landlord a specified portion of his crop and a certain number of days of work each year. The work allotment included not only the tenant himself, but services of all able-bodied members of his family. The system was typically feudal.

Outside of claiming ownership of Finland, the Czar left this northern duchy pretty much alone. The Finns had their own governing body, subject to the Czar, and their own languages, Swedish and Finnish, based upon an alphabet very different from the Russians, but the same as that of Western Europe.

Ethnically they appeared to be a mixture of Swedish descent, Balts from the Eastern Baltic regions, and an admixture of Hungarians, who had previously moved westward from the Ural mountain regions of old Russia.

Farming was the mainstay of the inhabitants, and on their lands they were largely self-sufficient. Large families were common, to offset high mortality rates among the young.

The Maki family, located on a tenant farm near the little town of Ikaalinen, was typical of the thousands of tillers of the soil. They raised their crops using horses and the simplest of farm implements: shovels, hoes, cradle scythes, and axes. The women worked beside the men planting, tending, and harvesting crops, and caring for livestock. A few cows and steers were kept for meat, milk, and cheese making. Flax was raised, then soaked for the manufacture of linen fiber which was later spun into yarn for cloth. Threshing of grain was done with a flail.

Inside the home, equipment was likewise quite primitive. There was a large fireplace with ovens built above each side for baking and roasting varieties of food. The spinning wheel stood nearby in frequent use, to make yarn which was later woven on a loom for clothing, bed sheets, tablecloths, or whatever was needed. Many hands and a lot of skills were required to accomplish both outside work and home duties in addition to laboring and producing what was owed to the landowner.

Tables and benches were bare of finish and were scrubbed with soap and lye until the birch wood was white. For baths, there was the sauna, or the lake nearby in warm weather.

The Makis went to church occasionally, sometimes with the team and wagon, but more often by sleigh or by boat across the lake to the Lutheran Church at Ikaalinen. When the children became old enough to attend school, they were boarded at homes in the village, as there were no countryside schools. They were taught basic reading, writing, and arithmetic for three or four years, and this completed their education. So the general picture of Finland and its people including the Maki family is complete.

However, since this family and its descendants are to play a major role as our story progresses, we must become better acquainted with them. Some will play only a minor part in our history. Others will, in their daily lives, move into familiar focus. They will become principal characters whose movements will be followed closely. And so their story begins.

Her first name was Ruusa. Soon after her first marriage, her husband fell from a boat and was drowned. Subsequently she remarried, this time to a man named Maki, first name unknown. There were eight children born of the second marriage; Nestor, Nikoteemu, Rosa, Josefina, Lydia, Ida, Sandra, and Frank. Nestor

7

was the oldest and Frank, the youngest. The order of birth of all of the girls is not available, but Lydia was born in eighteen hundred and eighty-one, followed by Ida and then Sandra. But since all were born rather close in age, it is surmised that they were born between eighteen hundred and seventy-five and eighteen hundred and eighty-five.

Each year, two weeks of Christmas were celebrated according to custom, after much preparation of food for the holidays and gathering of forage for the farm animals.

During the festivities all but the most necessary work was suspended. Visiting with neighbors, feasting, and several trips to church were the order of the times.

In summer the young folk would find an old derelict boat, boost it up on end near the lake shore, pile branches and wood around it. The pile was then set afire, and around the flames the couples would dance to the tunes of an accordion, until the fire died down.

At butchering time the men would build a large fire in a circle of rocks and place a barrel of water over it to heat, for scalding hogs, in order to loosen the bristles. After the slaughtering was completed, Lydia would take a potato out to the heated rocks. She would slice thin wafers from her potato and press them onto the rocks. They would cook through within a few minutes and came off dry and crisp. Then she would eat them. She didn't realize at the time that she was making what would later become known as potato chips.

In her turn she was sent to Ikaalinen to begin her studies. She attended school steadily for several months. But being one of the older siblings, she was called home often to help with the farm work. The chain of learning was interrupted, and finally she was not sent back at all. At home she would make serious efforts to continue learning to write. It was not enough. She drew, rather than wrote the words, even her name, with great effort. Soon she gave it up and went about the farm and household chores. The younger ones, Ida, Sandra, and Frank were allowed to continue in school, uninterrupted by farm duties, and they learned to read, to write well, and to handle arithmetic with ease.

The Makis were a healthy family. As with the Palms in Sweden, death did not claim any of the children.

There were no cripples or mentally retarded, a happy circumstance, but it created the same problem for the Makis as for the Palms. The farm and job situations were the same in Finland as in Sweden. Rumors of fabulous successes of emigrants in the United States were rampant. So it was circumstance that started members of the Maki family to begin their migration, the same condition which drove millions across the sea from other countries of Europe.

Nick, tall and muscular but quiet and taciturn by nature, was first to undertake the journey. Those who remained at home waited eagerly for his letters. They had heard often enough that Americans are rich and hoped that he would soon send them news of his success in the new country.

Their hopes were somewhat dashed when he finally wrote that he was living in a lumber camp cutting trees for one dollar a day and his keep. The letter savored of loneliness and of the desire to return home. This news had a sobering effect upon the family. They began to reassess the whole prospect of emigration. Eventually they decided that Nick's view of America was not real at all. It was characteristic of his negative view of everything. As time went by their spirits rose, and they began to dream bright dreams again. It was but a short time after Lydia's eighteenth birthday when her best friend Aune came rushing over to bring the news that she was leaving soon to go to the United States. She had borrowed the necessary funds, and knowing of Lydia's desire to go, urged that they travel together. Lydia had no money to make the trip overseas. She decided to try to get a loan from a prosperous neighbor, and soon after Aune left to return home, she called upon the prospective lender. He was slow to make up his mind, but he finally agreed to put up the money.

There followed a veritable whirlwind of preparation as clothing was made and preparations for the trip were completed. Lydia rushed to the lender's to complete arrangements for the loan, only to find that he had changed his mind and would not lend her the money after all.

In despair, she at first thought of giving up. But urged on by Aune, she applied to another man who agreed to the loan. This time the arrangements were completed and the money received.

As the time came for her departure, she clasped each one of the family to her breast. Smiling good-byes turned to tearful embraces. Would she ever see them again? She didn't know it at the time, but she would see the younger sisters and Frank the youngest brother. But she would not see her sister Rosa, her father, or mother again. Perhaps it is better that one is unable to see what lies in the future.

As the wagon started to move, she looked back at her relatives, gathered at the doorway. She waved them a final farewell. The horses trotted briskly toward Ikaalinen. "Americans are rich," she thought. "I'll get rich too and come back often to see my family." The journey to Ikaalinen passed swiftly.

Then there was Aune, and they boarded the stage for the port city of Turku. The boat was large. But it was no queen of the sea. It was a workhorse in need of paint, designed to carry as many immigrants as possible. The staterooms were tiny rectangular spaces holding two occupants. Aune and Lydia shared the same room, for which they were grateful, as they had not made previous reservations and indeed did not know such arrangements could be made.

The first leg of their journey brought them to Hull on the East coast of England. It would have been interesting to know their thoughts, what they did on this first part of the journey. Was the sea rough? Did they get seasick? The answers will remain unknown.

In port, they were taken with their luggage directly to a bus, which consisted of a long covered wagon with seats from front to back and with storage on the top for luggage. It was drawn by four horses.

They proceeded across the narrow waist of England to the port of Liverpool, with short stops for food and toiletries. There were no overnight delays. Passengers would catch up on sleep aboard the next ship after it set out from Liverpool.

This ship was much like the first, the small rooms crammed with immigrants from many nations. But there was a large space on deck. Evenings, when the weather permitted, there would be dancing to the music of a small orchestra. Couples waltzed and swayed until midnight, their movements often thwarted by those of the ship's rise and fall, as it plowed through, or rode a wave.

Looking at their tickets Lydia and Aune found that the ship's destination was Boston. They began trying to plan overland connections by rail; Aune to Philadelphia, and Lydia to Virginia, Minnesota, the closest town to where Nick worked in the logging camp.

They were surprised and their concern deepened when an elderly woman produced a map and pointed out the two locations, far apart and in different directions. Aune would have the shortest distance to travel. Looking at the map, Lydia was amazed to see the long distance she would have yet to travel.

Customs officials did not bother much about such poor immigrants as these but ushered them through the gates without searching their baggage.

Aune's train was scheduled to leave the railway station first. She had barely enough time to purchase her ticket. They embraced, and promised to write to each other, forgetting that addresses were needed, and as yet they had none to give. They would not see, or hear from each other again.

The ticket agent was patient but firm. After Lydia had placed her remaining money on the counter, he told her that she did not have enough for a ticket to Virginia, Minnesota. She finally decided that she would buy a ticket for as near to Virginia as the money would reach, saving out a few dollars for food. The ticket she could afford would take her as far as Sault St. Marie, Michigan. She boarded the train bewildered, lonely, and sick at heart. The train moved slowly at first, then gathered speed. Evening followed day. Then it was dark, and nothing could be seen through the coach window. Exhausted, Lydia slept fitfully, leaning against the dark window frame. Again it was day, and stopping occasionally at railway stations, the train hurried on. It was late in the afternoon when the conductor called Sault St. Marie as the next stop. Stiff and tired from the long ride, Lydia descended from the train with her baggage.

How she got her first job must go unrecorded. But almost immediately she was hired by an elderly gentleman to take care of his wife who was bedridden with cancer. The work also included cooking meals and keeping house for the couple who lived alone. But she was strong and a hard worker. At this point she must have taken stock of her situation and counted herself lucky. She had crossed the Atlantic to her new homeland, and the work, such as it was, would do for the present. There was much farther to go, but it could wait while she paid off her loan and could then save enough money for the final destination Virginia, Minnesota. The months went by and the old lady slowly weakened. It was necessary to feed her with a spoon, but she hung on tenaciously, fighting the inevitable. For Lydia, after a few weeks the work became routine. She seldom left the house, but looking through the window at women passing by she became conscious of their clothing, how different from that she had worn and brought along from Finland. Her dress would not do at all for this country. She spent her first month's salary for new dresses, stockings, and shoes. Wearing them for the first time, she was so proud that now she looked like other American women.

Her pleasure was short lived when, before her second month's pay was due, she received a scathing letter from the farmer who had made her the loan in Finland, informing her that she had not made any payments on her account. From that time until the loan was paid eight months later, her wages were remitted to the lender, with the required interest.

She began to save money again, hoping to continue her journey to Virginia. But the clothing she had purchased was now nearly worn out. It became necessary to buy several new outfits, a coat, sweater, and more shoes beside the under clothing and stockings to go with them. But her savings accumulated slowly.

Two more years went by, and she was twenty-one years old. The three years since her arrival in the United States had sped by unbelievably fast.

Ready at last, she sat by the window in the railway coach and watched the last buildings of Sault St. Marie slip backward in the distance. The year was 1902.

Presumably her trip to Virginia was much like the one that Charlie experienced in 1898, through the route to Duluth was a more northerly one, on the Soo line. Her story takes up again in Virginia, Minnesota.

The village consisted largely of small dwellings and shacks along a few uncertain roads curving around hills, ponds, and rocks. Westward from the railway depot, at the edge of a lake stood a large building housing a saw mill. The landscape was dotted with large pine stumps attesting to the fact that the area had once been covered by virgin pine forest. Eastward from the depot, blocks of homes were laid out in squares, with streets unpaved, often totally unimproved except for the main street which was paved with blocks of wood or brick. Much of the town gave one the impression of an overgrown lumber camp. But Main street was filling up with hotels, bars, and stores dispensing clothing, groceries, and hardware.

For all its rude ugliness there was a cosmopolitan atmosphere about the place. Its inhabitants had arrived from many countries of Europe. They brought with them their languages, their customs, their religious preferences, and all of the various mystiques of native lands beyond the Atlantic. At first there was a strong tendency for them to segregate themselves by language, nationality, and religion. The fusion process was slow.

It was into this scene that Lydia stepped from the train in the late spring of 1902. Her brother was at the station to meet her. He had found a place for her to room in the home of a Finnish family. She was happy to see him again. He was taller and more mature. Gathering her luggage, they walked the few blocks to her new home, just off of Main Street. Over luncheon in a nearby restaurant, they explored the possibilities for her first job application. It was decided that to start with, she could do well working as a chambermaid at a hotel, because of her experience working with the cancer patient at Sault St. Marie.

Leaving the restaurant they elected to begin with the Svea Hotel. Mrs. Carlson wasted no time in hiring Lydia to start the following morning. Her duties were to clean rooms, make beds, and help with the laundry. As they left the hotel, she could hardly believe that events of her life could arrange themselves so speedily. It was necessary for her to return to her room and prepare her clothes for work. Nick left at her door, promising to return the following Sunday.

Mrs. Carlson was like a second mother to her employees and to the men who stayed at the Svea Hotel. She took time to speak a few cheery words to everyone, to listen to a problem, or hear a joke. It was her personality and her kind disposition that made the Svea a good place stay. In return, she was loved by those in her charge.

Lydia learned her duties quickly and carried them out thoroughly. She and Mrs. Carlson became good friends. On Sundays, Nick would come to take her out for a quick luncheon at a restaurant, and they would stroll down Main Street. It was on one of these walks that he told her of his decision to return to Finland. Another person in his place would have made a hearty transition. It was perhaps in his brooding character that the answer lay. They had two more Sunday walks together, then he was gone. Lydia began to feel lonely herself.

Notwithstanding Nick's departure, letters arrived across the sea from Ida and Sandra, filled with accounts of their desires and their preparations to come to Virginia. Lydia's answering letters were encouraging, and she began to look forward to their arrival the following summer. Time passed and it was the spring of 1903.

CHAPTER III

The Iron Range

One day Charlie walked into the lobby of the Svea Hotel, and Mrs. Carlson was standing at the counter. "Come with me Charlie, "I she said "There is someone I want you to meet." She led him back into the laundry where Lydia was ironing bed sheets.

"Charlie, this is Lydia Maki. Lydia, this is Charlie Palm," she said. The introduction acknowledged, Charlie turned to Mrs. Carlson. "My name is Palmer now instead of Palm. You see, when I went to work for the company, the supervisor asked for my name, and I said it was Palm. He told me that I couldn't be Palm because they already had two Palms working there, a big fellow that they called Big Palm and a small one that they called Little Palm, so he said my name is Palmer." They laughed. Then he asked Lydia, "What does Maki mean in Finnish?" " It is the same as Hill in English," she replied. Mrs. Carlson left them to visit while Lydia kept ironing sheets on the ironing board, stopping occasionally to get a heated iron from the stove.

On the Sunday afternoons that followed, Charlie and Lydia could be seen riding to Eveleth with a rented horse and buggy. They had a favorite restaurant there that served oyster stew. It was probably on one of those jaunts that they became engaged to be married.

Mrs. Carlson had a problem, or rather a series of problems. No sooner did she find a good chambermaid, but some miner or logger would snatch her away in marriage. Now it was Lydia about to marry Charlie and Mrs. Carlson was in a stew about it. She would lose them both of course, but could she delay their plans? When they came in from their ride, she faced them.

"If you wait with your marriage for six months, I will give you the whole wedding free," she explained. They were surprised at the offer. After talking it over, they decided to accept. So Mrs. Carlson kept her maid and her boarder for another six months, and the rides to Eveleth continued.

Meanwhile Charlie was transferred to the shops in Mountain Iron. He had to commute every day via street car to his job. The last five years had wrought quite a change in his appearance. There was the new black serge suit, the bowler hat for regular wear, and the flat brimmed round top for dress. But the change appeared more in his personality than in the clothes he wore. There was an air of confidence, of self-assurance about him. He was a mature man, speaking the new English language fluently, albeit with somewhat of a Swedish lilt.

For Lydia the wedding delay was in a way fortunate. She began sewing dresses and other clothing for herself. What money she could spare went for table cloths, bedding, and other household linen. About a week before the wedding, Charlie rented a small house near the trolley line.

Mrs. Carlson, as good as her word, furnished the complete wedding and the large reception that followed. There was quite a large gathering of friends, hotel guests, and staff at the church, and afterward at the hotel. Finally Charlie and Lydia slipped away to their first home. The next day there were wedding pictures to be taken at the photographers with Charlie sitting on a bench and Lydia in her white wedding dress standing beside him, her elbow resting on his shoulder. Looking out of the pictures, their expressions were calm and serious.

Spring, then summer, then fall went swiftly by, and it was cold again. There were more letters from Finland. Ida and Sandra were still making plans to immigrate. Now they had decided to bring Frank, the younger brother, with them. Letters began arriving from a new quarter. Charlie's brother Axel wrote that he would be coming soon. But there was a problem. Fred, Werner, and Anna wanted to come with him. They were so young and what

Wedding picture of Charlie and Lydia Palmer, 1905.

would the old folks do in Sweden without them? The months went by and nothing was settled.

On February 20th of nineteen hundred and six, Lydia gave birth to a healthy, fat baby girl. They named her Lillian Marie. There was a baptism and another round of photographs to be taken.

A new Singer treadle sewing machine was on the market but few families owned one. Lydia hand stitched Lillian's dresses and underclothes, dreaming of the day when she would have a sewing machine. But she was happy when Charlie brought home the washing stand with a clothes wringer in the middle. Now, after the water was heated on the stove, she could fill one tub with fresh water, and rub the clothes on a scrubbing board before running them through the wringer into the tub of rinse water on the other side. It was a wonderful invention, used daily, and then the cleaned but wet wash had to be hung outside on the clothesline. In winter it would freeze solid in a few minutes. But it would dry overnight and become soft and flexible again by morning. Washing, cooking, housecleaning, and sewing soon became a normal routine in the little rented house.

Meanwhile, at the shop, Charlie listened to news about larger iron ore deposits in the Hibbing area forty miles west, and of gigantic operations planned to mine them. New repair shops would be built, and opportunities for advancement in them would be much better than in Virginia. Several mechanics who had already moved to Hibbing sent back optimistic accounts about the expanding operation. Charlie began to get itchy feet. He stepped from the train in Hibbing one Sunday morning to see for himself what the mining operations were like. What he saw convinced him that his chances for advancement in the railroad shops would be much greater in Hibbing. But he found that housing was scarce. He boarded the street car for Chisholm, a small village about nine miles northeast of Hibbing, and located some empty homes in Hartly location, a small suburb. The houses were small. They all stood on posts above the ground. Water was carried from a community pump located near the center of the cluster of houses.

The setup would do for a temporary home until a place could be found in Hibbing, but Charlie would have to travel again to and from work by street car. He decided to accept this inconvenience because he was already travelling in the same fashion to and from Mountain Iron. Back in Virginia he told Lydia of his decision to move.

He arrived the next morning in the Hibbing shop office of the Winston and Deere Mining Company. Seated at the desk was an enormously fat, large-jowled man, who asked Charlie for his name and introduced himself as H. C. Hansen. He waived Charlie to a chair, seated himself behind the desk once more, and began to ask about Charlie's experience in shop work, meanwhile offering a cigar and clipping the end off another for himself with a clipper attached to an enormous watch chain across his chest. He spoke English well but with an accent that proclaimed his Danish ancestry. His slow deliberate manner did not disclose the fact that he was desperately short of good shop mechanics. Charlie left the office with his new job of mechanic and with the promise of time to move his family to the environs of Hibbing. Speedily, he rented one of the houses in Hartly location and returned to Virginia.

There was a flurry of packing the household belongings and then unpacking them at the new home. The new location was not a pretty site. It was situated on a hill denuded of trees by loggers. Wind swept under the houses making the floors cold. It was fall, and they would soon be colder.

Life began again in the new surroundings, and a routine of work was re-established. It was supposed to be temporary, but they would remain in the Hartly location for more than a year. With the coming of winter, drafts filtered through the walls and the floors were always cold. Finally Lydia came down with typhoid fever and took to her bed sweating and so weak she could not feed herself. Charlie became the cook and had to feed her with a spoon. He washed the clothes and cared for baby Lillian. They were quarantined. So there was no question of his going to work. Finally Lydia's fever dropped, and she began to recover. Meanwhile Lillian seemed to thrive on her father's cooking and the cold floors. She was walking and getting into all kinds of mischief. Then Lydia was up and about and Charlie returned to his job. Winter wore on and the snow began to melt.

One day, Lydia came in from hanging clothes on the line to find Lillian standing on the sideboard of the kitchen cabinet. She had climbed upon it from a chair and had reached for a pretty bottle, taken it down and was drinking the contents which were half gone when Lydia entered. The bottle contained wine. Hurriedly Lydia lifted her from the sideboard and not knowing what else to do, put her to bed where she immediately fell asleep. Lydia spent several anxious hours before Lillian awakened apparently unharmed by the wine. Thereafter it was placed away beyond her reach.

One night Lydia and Charlie were awakened by a strange knocking and banging under the house. They lay awake trying to figure out the cause of the noise. Finally Charlie got out of bed, dressed, and taking a flashlight, went out to investigate. Under the house was a skunk, and he had gotten his head stuck in a snuff jar, which he was banging around trying to get his head free. Luckily, the skunk did not become afraid, so he didn't let loose his spray. Charlie went back to bed, which turned out to be the best thing to do. In the morning the skunk was gone, leaving the snuff jar behind.

Charlie had an emergency job at the shop one day. One of the locomotives had broken a wheel bearing and there were no spare bearings to replace it. H. C. Hansen, they called him "H. C.", was in a stew. A locomotive out of action would hold up the job of stripping the surface dirt away from the iron ore. He asked Charlie if there was something he could do. Charlie told him that the bearing could not be fixed, but that he thought he could make a new one. H. C. looked at him in amazement but told him to go ahead and try.

It would be a long process, and Charlie knew it. He stripped the bearing housing from the shaft and cleaned away broken bits of old bearing. Then the housing had to be fitted to the shaft again with veins of putty, and heated babbitt was poured into this makeshift mold. When the babbitt was cold, it was pounded off the end of the shaft and the putty was removed. When it was cleaned up, the new bearing was mounted on the shaft. When H. C. returned the next morning, the locomotive stood in the shop yards with steam up, ready to go to work. "Charlie, you aren't a mechanic any more; you're a master mechanic, " he said looking at Charlie with a smile. Charlie grinned with appreciation. The night's work had brought him a promotion. His was a special mechanical mind, and H. C. knew it. From this time they would become close friends. H. C. would come again and again with shop problems, and together, most of the time the problems would get solved.

Being a master mechanic meant that Charlie would often have to work long past the regular quitting time. Usually he was able to leave the shop in time to catch the last streetcar that left for Chisholm at eleven o'clock in the late evening. But one night it was nearly midnight when his work was finished. He decided to walk home. The night was dark, and somehow he lost his way. Suddenly he was falling and sliding downward in the darkness. Finally, the soil leveled out underfoot. On his knees, he felt of the ground. There was soft iron ore underfoot. He had fallen into the open iron ore pit. At length he located the train tracks leading upwards out of the mine and followed them back to the surface. This time he was more careful in choosing his homeward route. He followed the streetcar tracks to Chisholm, and the lighted street to Hartley location. Disgusted with this experience, he began an intensive search for housing in Hibbing. There was talk among the miners of a new housing development called Pool location.

By fall the Palmers were already relocated there, and none to soon for Lydia was again big with child. She was more content in her new home because it was larger, there were no drafts blowing through the walls, and there was water piped right into the kitchen sink. How handy, how efficient, and modern, and she had at last been able to persuade Charlie to buy a treadle Singer sewing machine. Moreover, they had made many good friends in the

21

neighborhood, the Neumans, the Arnbecks, the Johnsons, and many others. Their second child, a boy, was born soon afterward on January 26, nineteen hundred and eight. They named him Axel Fredrick after Charlie's brother.

They now lived close enough to the repair shops so that Charlie could walk to and from work. Pool location was situated in a grove of trees. It was but a short distance to Hibbing proper and there was the continual sound of hammering and sawing as more houses took shape. A library and a large school building were going up, and there were plans for a courthouse and city hall. There were rumors that the whole village was being constructed on top of a rich, enormous pocket of ore, but construction continued regardless.

CHAPTER IV

Family Matters

Lydia was laboriously writing letters to Virginia, Minnesota because Ida, Sandra, and Frank had arrived there from Finland. Ida and Sandra found work immediately in Virginia while Frank moved eastward to Tower where he was engaged in the lumber business. The sisters, in their off hours, were sewing new clothes. They wrote with great excitement of going to dances and hinted that they were already going steady with beaus. Lydia was anxious to go to see them, but the new baby, the washing, and housekeeping kept her tied down.

Meanwhile there was a stream of importuning letters arriving from Ljungby in Sweden. Axel wrote that Fred, Werner, and Anna insisted on coming to America. It was unthinkable that they should leave the old folks at home alone. Old Fredrick was no longer able to work the farm, and Sarah hobbled about using a cane to ease her ailing hip. The old pair puttered around bewildered and uncertain over leaving their home in Berga. Faced with being uprooted from familiar ground, they seemed to abdicate all responsibility and passed their authority on to the children.

Fred, Werner, and Anna were teenagers so the responsibility fell squarely on the shoulders of Charlie and Axel. They decided to sell the farm in Sweden, bring the whole family across, and settle them on a newly purchased farm in Turtle Lake, Wisconsin, close to some friends who had moved several years previously. Hindsight told them that it would have been better to have waited a few years before making the change, but at the time they could not have foreseen the difficulties their decision would hatch.

23

When the folks arrived and were established on the farm west of Turtle Lake, it was already far into the growing season, which meant that they would have to be supplied with food and clothing for a while. Axel came to Hibbing and got a job in the mines to keep them supplied, and Charlie sent money at intervals to help and to purchase a team of horses, a cow, and some farm tools. Old Fredrick seemed to retire and leave the farming to his children. But Sarah went on with the cooking and washing with her old vigor, moving about with the cane ever thumping beside her.

Fred, Werner, and Anna were used to being told what to do. But with Axel and Charlie away and old Fredrick in a state of abdication, they seemed unable to assume responsibility and did little to prepare for winter. Suddenly letters began arriving in Hibbing saying, "We are cold, we are freezing." It was necessary for Charlie to take several days off from work and make a trip out to the farm. He found them huddled around the stove burning scraps of wood gathered from the farmyard. There was a large grove of trees on the farm. Charlie hitched the team of horses to the wagon and got Werner and Fred started cutting firewood. Fred complained that his thumbs were double jointed and that he couldn't use an axe. Charlie didn't let him get by with that excuse and soon had him chopping wood like a veteran lumberjack. Fred was hot tempered, often quarrelsome and negative. It seemed that he would never mature or accept responsibility for anything, himself included. Charlie returned to Hibbing with the heating problem solved.

Early the following spring, Fred came to Hibbing to visit and to see the mines and the shops. Charlie was showing him some locomotives newly purchased by the company when H. C. Hansen emerged from his office and joined them. When their inspection was finished, H. C. said, "Yah, now if I only had some engineers to run them." Charlie thought a moment, then pointed to Fred. "I think he can do it," he said. H. C. looked the skinny young man up and down. Then he said, "OK, Charlie if you think you can teach him, go ahead."

24

Fred caught on to the intricacies of running a locomotive quickly and became an engineer, a vocation that was to be his until many years later when he retired.

With Fred working, Werner, in his middle teens was for all practical purposes left to run the farm in Turtle Lake alone. Old Fredrick had ceased working except to putter around the farm yard. Axel hastened there in the spring to help put in the crops. There by chance he met Anna Peterson and romance began to flourish. The crops in, he returned to his job in Hibbing but his trips to Turtle Lake became frequent.

Meanwhile in Hibbing, since Lydia could not seem to get over to see her sisters in Virginia, Ida decided to visit her in Hibbing. Charlie was supposed to meet her at the train depot. He wanted to clean up and change clothes before going to the station, but last minute duties kept him at the shop until it was almost time for the train to arrive. So, clad in his dirty and greasy clothes, his face covered with black grime, he stood on the railway platform as the passengers began to descend from the coach. He recognized Ida from pictures he had seen of her. However, when he approached her, she stepped back, alarmed by this filthy stranger who had dared to step up in such a familiar fashion. She could hardly speak a word of English. But he kept saying, "Ida" and "Lydia" and she became confused. Finally Charlie lifted her suitcase from the platform and motioning for her to follow, started walking toward home. She followed but would not walk beside him. "This could not be Charlie!" she thought. Finally there was Lydia standing in the front yard waiting for her, and they rushed into each other's arms, jabbering meanwhile in their native Finnish Language. While they caught up on the news, Charlie bathed and put on his best suit, the one that he had purchased for sixteen dollars and that "wore like iron." He emerged from the bathroom a different man, face scrubbed, showing that perfect set of teeth in a broad smile. With Lydia translating they had a conversation of sorts, and Ida began to conceive a liking for the demon who first met her at the depot.

The news Ida brought was that she was engaged to a miner

too, but he wanted to become a farmer and a logger. He was searching for a piece of land near Cook to set his plans in motion. The young brother, Frank, was working at a mill in Tower during the winter months, and in summer he was busy towing rafts of logs from forested areas around Lake Vermillion to stockpile for sawing during the time when the lake was frozen over.

Her brief visit concluded, Ida returned to Virginia leaving Lydia with a sense of lonesomeness for her old family. "Little by little we will drift apart into lives of our own, and it will never ~e the same again," she thought. Time would prove her thoughts correct, though the sisters kept in touch with letters and occasional short trips to visit one another.

Lydia and Charlie wanted to get out and socialize. To do that it was necessary to join a club, go to dances or join a church, to meet people somehow. They didn't care for church, though Lydia had her children baptized, saying "It's best to be sure." The Odd Fellows Lodge seemed the best avenue of approach, since dances were held regularly at the lodge hall and Charlie loved to dance, so they joined. They were sitting in the dance hall, and the musicians, after tuning up began to play a waltz. Lydia, unsure of how she would perform in this new atmosphere said that she wanted to watch a while first, so Charlie looked about for another partner. Spying one to his liking he approached her and asked her to be his partner for the dance. She said, "No thank you, I prefer an introduction."

Undaunted, Charlie searched further and soon found a lady that turned out to be a very good dancer. As they whirled about in the waltz, Charlie imagined the wine glass on his head back in Chicago. He felt a light touch on his arm. It was the lady who had turned him down on the ground of not having an introduction. "I'll dance with you," she called. Charlie twirled back toward her and answered, "No thanks, I prefer an introduction." In recounting this incident he never did say whether the lady ever got her dance with him. So the social life began. Friendships developed in many places, from the grocery stores to the mines and repair shops.

Then it was 1909 and Lydia was carrying a child again She

settled down to caring for Lillian and Axel and to wait for the next one to arrive.

Things were not going well at the farm at Turtle Lake. Old Fredrick was ailing and Werner could not handle the work. He was too young. Charlie and Axel began to doubt the wisdom of having bought the farm in the first place. They knew it was a good productive piece of property, but things had just not worked out as they had planned. But for the time being nothing was done. Axel continued his frequent trips to Turtle Lake, ostensibly to check on the crops. However, much of the time he could be seen over at the Peterson's farm courting Anna.

The country was experiencing a financial depression in the early nineteen hundreds. Everyone agreed that it was a temporary phase that would soon change back to normal. Instead of laying off men the mining companies began issuing script instead of money. The script was honored by both banks and stores. Business went on as usual, except that it created a problem for one man, H. C. Hansen.

Since this remarkable giant of a man was to play an important role in the lives of the Palmer family and a considerable part in the history of Hibbing as well, his living portrait deserves clear delineation. It has been related that he came to the Hibbing area about the time that iron was first discovered there. He started a small logging operation, and it grew into a considerable enterprise. His wife took in washing from the lumberjacks at first and generally helped her husband with his accounts. With the first recession H. C. was caught with large amounts owing for equipment and wages, but there was no market for his logs, and his business was wiped out.

He started again with a small logging operation, and his wife resumed washing clothes for the loggers. Gradually the recession ended, and once more he prospered. But then his wife died.

It is not known what effect this had upon his change into the mining field. As a logger he had been highly ethical in his procurement of stumpage for tree cutting, unlike some others who would buy a forty acre plot for cutting trees and the log then country for miles around it. He made a name for himself as a man of integrity among the leaders of Hibbing.

It is probable that he was offered the superintendent's position for Winston and Deere because of his solid reputation. Then too, he could handle men. They liked his slow unruffled manner of giving orders and conducting business.

His problem was concerned with another matter. Since his first wife's death, he had been a lonely man. Then one day he met a woman that jolted him out of his quiet, solitary existence, and he fell in love with her. She accepted his marriage proposal, but he couldn't buy engagement or wedding rings with company script which was accepted only in Hibbing. No jewelry store in Duluth would honor it. Stopping in at the repair shops one day, he saw Charlie hammering away at a piece of iron bar. The idea clicked in his brain. Charlie was a saver! Could it be that he would have enough saved to buy rings? He called Charlie and asked him to come to the office. After the usual banalities, H. C. asked Charlie if he could lend him five hundred dollars.

Charlie blinked a few times but maintained his composure. It happened that he had just a little more than that amount hidden away in his suitcase at home. "Yes, I can lend it to you, but I must go home and get it," he said. "Never mind, bring it tomorrow. I'll give you a note for it," H. C. replied. As Charlie left the office, H. C. chuckled. The problem of the rings was solved, and yes, he had read Charlie right. The following day H. C. boarded the train for Duluth on some business with a jeweler.

The snow lay four inches deep in Hibbing. It covered the houses in Pool location and the ground under the trees of the nearby grove since it had fallen one night two weeks before. Charlie wandered aimlessly out among the trees and discovered rabbit tracks there, literally by the thousands. "This country must be teeming with rabbits," he thought. "If I had a shotgun, we could have baked rabbit whenever we wished." The next step was obvious. "I've got to buy a shotgun."

The hardware man showed Charlie his stock of guns and the best one, a Remington pump action, took his eye. Home with his new gun, he could hardly wait until Sunday and some good hunting. He was out early on Sunday morning and bagged two snowshoe hares. He gutted and skinned them, and Lydia promised to have them ready for supper on Monday night.

Sunday evening it snowed again. They had baked rabbit for supper Monday evening. After that Charlie went out again to see if there were more rabbit tracks in the new snow. But he never found any. Those two rabbits must have made all those tracks by themselves!

The recession was finally over, and currency was again in full flow. H. C.'s wedding was a grand affair, and most of his friends and Hibbing's elite were at the church. His big home was open to all for the reception which followed. The festivities over, he closed the door and embraced his new bride. He hoped that he would soon have the son he yearned for.

November passed and on the first day of December, 1909 Lydia presented Charlie with another son. They named him Charles after his father and Victor after no other relative. He was duly baptized at the Lutheran Church with Lydia's good friend Ellen Newman as Godmother. With three children the household work increased. There was little time for dances and parties.

Hibbing continued to grow and expand in all directions until geological engineers began taking test core samples of the under-lying soil. The samples revealed that the entire village rested over a gigantic body of high grade iron ore. There was talk among the city officials to moving the village southward two miles where tests indicated only clay and rock under the surface. A new town was plotted on paper in the event of such a move. The plot completed, all building ceased in the original village, and con-struction began in the new area. Some homes were torn down and rebuilt on hastily purchased lots two miles south. Many owners decided to jack their homes up, put them on rollers, and trundle them to the new village in one piece. Soon H. C.'s house was on rollers inching southward with the others.

The mining company began buying up lots from individual householders, to the consternation of their neighbors. They began to visualize their homes balanced on a pillar of iron ore out in the middle of an open chasm. So they gathered together in blocks to protect their interests against depredation by the mining interests. For those who moved two miles south, getting to work became a problem. It was a long walk to and from work each day.

One day two young men who loved to tinker with the newfangled automobiles and trucks that began to appear on the roads, were looking at a long bedded truck standing by their garage. They talked about the possibility of putting a roof over the truck bed and placing seats to carry passengers.

So Anderson, later nicknamed "bus Andy" and Mr. Hogan went to work on the truck to carry out their idea. When the job was completed, they placed their bus in service carrying passengers between North and South Hibbing. The demand for this service rose so sharply that they soon had a fleet of buses in operation. Later, routes were established to other towns on the Iron Range and to Duluth. At first, each bus carried the name "Blue Goose" painted on its side. That was later changed to "Greyhound Bus Lines." It was the beginning of what was to become the nationally famous Greyhound Line. But that was in the future.

H. C. Hansen stood by the shop door and watched a saddleback engine pushing a string of railroad cars loaded with surface strippings up the dump incline. When the cars reached the end of the track, a man went from car to car and cranked the box tiltwise to let its cargo of dirt slide out and down the side of the dump. It bothered him, this slow tedious process of dumpinq. "The car brakes are set by air pressure," he thought. "Why can't they all be dumped at once by air pressure?" He strolled over to a dump car parked on a siding and began to examine the construction of its dumping mechanism. Gradually the idea of an invention for dumping the cars by air pressure formed in his mind.

Once the idea was on paper, he consulted with a patent attorney, and the patent application was on its way to Washington, D. C. He received a notice about two months later that his patent had been granted. He began receiving offers almost immediately from manufacturers who wanted to build the dumping mechanism. Then royalties began to arrive in the mail. He was amazed to find that his invention was being installed on dump cars throughout the whole United States. Once again he was on his way to becoming a wealthy man. He wanted to buy one of those new gasoline automobiles but found that he could not drive one, just couldn't get the hang of it. Finally he hired a man who could double as a gardener and chauffeur, furnished him with a uniform for driving and bought a large black straight eight Packard.

Meanwhile his wife gave birth to a beautiful blonde baby girl. For some unknown reason, she never became pregnant again, so his hopes for a son were dashed. Strange that his brother could have three healthy sons and he had none. But nephews were the same as sons in a way. After all, his blood and his brother's blood were the same, and his name would continue to carry on. It was an idea.

South Hibbing mushroomed until it was as large as North Hibbing, then surpassed it. The new town boasted wider streets, newly paved, a finer layout plan, and better schools. There were jobs going begging. No expense was spared to buy city lights and equipment.

Property taxes were very low because the mining companies paid about ninety-five percent of taxes levied and homeowners paid the remaining five percent. It was a golden age in which to live, and the iron ore would last for a hundred years at least, according to the best estimates of company engineers.

With the new baby, he was called "Victor," so as not to be confuse things by having two Charlies, Lydia was washing almost continuously. Charlie brought home a new kind of washing machine one day. It consisted of a wooden tub mounted on legs. There was a handle sticking up on one side of the tub, and when it was pushed back and forth, an agitator in the bottom of the tub would shove the clothes around in hot water and soap suds. "It is a wonderful invention," thought Lydia. "These Americans, what they won't think of next?" When not washing, she cleaned the house and cooked. Cooking became her favorite chore, and it developed from a chore into a source of enjoyment and pleasure.

Mr. James who lived a few houses away was killed in a mining accident leaving a widow and five children. Lydia watched the children from her window as they passed each day on their way to school. She wondered if they had enough to eat. Frequently Charlie would come home to find five extra little urchins at his table for supper. He understood his wife's anxiety for the neighbor's children, and it gave him satisfaction to see them eagerly cleaning up the food on their plates. Test cores taken under the soil at Pool location confirmed engineer's suspicions that under it lay a massive deposit of iron ore. Eventually the settlement would have to be moved. There was considerable speculation as to how soon this would happen.

CHAPTER V

Railroads

John D. Rockefeller had succeeded in taking over the railroad between Virginia and Duluth from the Merrit brothers. Plans for a branch line were completed to hook into the main railway at Alborn and across northwestward to Coleraine and the western end of the Iron Range. This branch to be named the Duluth, Mesabi, and Iron Range Railway. The builders received the usual right-of-way plus ownership of every other section of land through which the rails traversed. Speedily the roadbed was prepared and the rails nailed in place. As a result ore production in the western area of the Iron Range grew by leaps and bounds. Iron ore tonnage shipped on the western branch would easily pay for the costs of the new railroad. It crossed straight as an arrow through timber, swamp, and sand hills uninhabited except for a few Indians, a few hardy Swedish families who had moved up the St. Louis and Whiteface rivers by canoe to build their homes high on the riverbanks, a few trappers after the dwindling fur bearing animals, and here and there a solitary lumberjack turned squatter, left behind when the pine forests near the rivers were harvested to be floated downstream to the mills in Cloquet. Through this wilderness, the Whiteface and St. Louis rivers meandered westward, then southward, and finally eastward toward Duluth from the Mesabi Range. Gathering runoff from smaller streams, becoming wider and deeper, they wended their way gradually closer until the Whiteface spilled into the St. Louis and lost its identity in the larger stream. Steam locomotives hauling strings of railroad cars heaped with heavy iron ore used a lot of water enroute from the mines to the ore docks in Duluth. A large water tank was constructed on a platform by the Whiteface River bridge to refill the locomotive tanks. By the tracks one mile northwest of the water tank a small station was constructed. The area as yet had no townsite nor any name, though the few Swedish farms by the river went by the unofficial designation of "Swedetown."

Now that the railroad had been completed the railway officials began to make plans to market the adjoining land grants along the right of way. They knew little of the soil composition except under the road bed. A land agency was established to locate the most promising sites for settlements adjacent to the railway, to survey and platt village areas and to construct railway sidings where box cars could be shunted off the main tracks to bring in building materials and load timber from the forests. One of the sites chosen was close to the small railway station not far from the Whiteface river water tank. For sales promotional purposes they named this bit of wilderness "Meadowlands," though there were as yet no meadows visible. An intense advertising campaign was launched to promote land sales. Gradually the forests receded, stumps were blasted from the soil or they were pulled out with horses. A small meadow did indeed begin to appear. A store was erected near the depot, and a house nearby for its owner. The next building to appear was a one room school, southwestward among the poplar trees.

CHAPTER VI

The New Horizons

Back in Hibbing, Lydia, Charlie, and their three children were carrying on as before. Victor was now one and a half years old. Another round of pictures was taken at the photographers. Lydia had made a short trip to Virginia to attend the wedding of Ida to her sweetheart, Hans. Soon afterward the newlyweds moved to Keewatin, a small mining community twenty miles west of Hibbing. Then Sandra and August were married which called for another trip to Virginia and another round of festivities. August was not cut out to be a miner. He wanted to be a farmer in the summer and a logger in the winter. Searching the surrounding countryside, he finally located a piece of land near Gheen, about forty-five miles north of Virginia that seemed ideal for his plans. From the timber on his newly acquired land, he constructed a large two-story house, a barn, and of course, a sauna. Sandra milked cows and kept the homework going while he was away logging in winter.

Lydia, Ida, and Sandra received letters from Frank in Tower that he too was married, to which they returned their congratulations and wished happiness to the newlyweds. However, they were somewhat disappointed in not being able to attend the wedding and fuss over their "Baby" brother.

Charlie's brother Fred, in his off hours from running locomotives, spent much of his time down at the bus depot watching the passengers boarding and leaving buses, talking with "Bus" Andy or just loafing. He seemed to have no interest in women. He didn't dance, drink, or chew snuff but he liked to argue about almost anything.

Charlie and Axel would stop at the bar of the Anderson Hotel occasionally after work for a beer. There was a moose head mounted on the wall opposite to the bar. High on the back wall a stuffed lynx bared his fangs and glared at a fearless two headed calf. Long familiar with these monstrosities, the brothers gave them small attention.

The farm situation in Turtle Lake was no better, but Axel reported progress in his courtship of Anna Peterson. He was thinking seriously of quitting his job in the mines to buy a farm for himself and Anna, after they married, in the Turtle Lake area. Walking home, Charlie worried over the news that old Fredrick, his father, was failing in health, that it was only a matter of time.

One day a lady who taught school in the Hibbing grade school walked into the Johnson grocery and hardware store. Seeing Mr. Johnson behind the counter, she approached and said, "I'd like to buy some pecans." Mr. Johnson answered, "Sure, Ma'am, large, medium, or small?" The lady seemed confused by his question, so he retired into the back storeroom and soon reappeared with three sizes of chamber pots. Hibbing chuckled from one end to the other as this story passed from ear to mouth, the choicest of gossip.

Lydia was watching little Axel as he played in the yard. He stumbled over something and fell down. Then he got up and turned around. Backing up to see what he had stumbled over, he tripped over another obstacle and down he went again. Lydia chuckling, thought, "When will he learn to look where he's going?"

The H. C. Hansens often went for drives in the countryside around Hibbing. The chauffeur received orders to follow this road or that or to stop at some point of interest. Little Hazel, two years old, her flaxen hair flying about her face was worshipped by both Mama and Daddy.

H. C. was a farmer at heart, a throwback to his Danish parentage. As they travelled, he examined the passing landscape. Possibilities for farming here were poor indeed; the soil was suitable only for forest land. It would be necessary to find a better location than this to carry out his plans for a farm. Beside the good salary he received from Winston and Deere, royalties from the car dumping patent increased year by year. He was already a wealthy man, easily able to diversify and invest in other projects.

Reading the Hibbing Tribune at the office one June morning an article caught his attention. It was a description of a big land development project about to be launched at a place called Meadowlands, adjacent to the Duluth, Mesabi, and Iron Range Railroad. He studied the article closely and phoned his lawyer. "How about us going for a drive out to see this new land development project?" he asked.

The road to Meadowlands was little more than a trail, but they made the journey in about two hours. What they saw when they reached the development were but the bare bones of a town, a small general store, one house standing nearby, and a small railway station. Carpenters were busy constructing a long tenement house, and on the side track loggers were busy loading timber onto some flat cars. H. C. stopped the automobile several times to kick up some soil under the grass and the trees. It looked good, black, and fertile, and it was on high ground. There were no swamps visible.

H. C. gave his lawyer instructions to buy up some lots in the townsite. Then he located a one hundred and sixty acre tract about one half mile northwestward, along the tracks, and ordered the lawyer to purchase that also. They stopped to talk with the proprietor of the store. Mr. McMaster told them that business was slow, that he might sell out, and move on. H. C. gave him his card and told him to write if he ever decided to sell.

H. C. was exhilarated during the drive back to Hibbing. He gloried in having a new project going again. Within six months the land purchases were completed; the store and the home beside it were acquired. A large barn and house were almost completed on the farmland. A Mr. Albertson was brought in from North Dakota to run the farm. Mr. McMaster was to turn over the store at the end of six months.

Meanwhile there was the problem of finding a manager to take over the store when it was vacated. H. C. had for some time been mulling over various ideas to help his three nephews. Axel, the eldest, recently married to Nora, was a clerk in one of the mining offices. Jobs like that never led anywhere. H. C. began to consider him as a possible manager. True, he was quite young. Perhaps if he had a partner, a steady more mature man with him in the enterprise, there would be more certainty of its success. In his thoughts H. C. cast about among his acquaintances trying to settle upon someone suitable. Charlie Palmer cropped up in his mind several times, but Charlie was doing well in his job of master mechanic. H. C. continued to search for other candidates. There seemed to be no one else, so he began to reassess the possibility of offering Charlie a full partnership in the store. As Meadowlands grew, the business could become a highly profitable venture. The merchants would become prosperous within a few years. True, they had no retail experience, but that could be learned in a short time.

His decision made, H. C. sent one of the clerks out to the shop to bring Charlie in for a chat.

CHAPTER VII

The Decision

That night Lydia listened as Charlie outlined H. C.'s offer. The impact of such a drastic change in their lives was mind boggling. To move out into a wilderness, leaving their friends and to start anew in an unfamiliar business venture seemed to Lydia a very risky move. Charlie was secure in his job in Hibbing, and the paychecks came in regularly. At bedtime they were decisionless, completely bewildered, but they were tired and sleep stole swiftly in, erasing all of their thoughts.

A week went by, and they began to get used to the idea of moving to Meadowlands. In another week it began to take on the aura of an exciting adventure. Charlie went in on the following Monday morning to notify H. C. that he would accept the offer.

Lydia had sewn a new dress for Lillian and a suit each for Axel and Victor. She was very proud of her work on the new treadle Singer sewing machine. She dressed the children in their new clothes, and off they went to the studio for a group photograph. Lydia liked the resulting picture of the three children seated on a bench, so she ordered several extra copies to send to Ida, Sandra, and Frank.

She had forebodings concerning the move to Meadowlands but when she mentioned them to Charlie, he told her not to worry that everything would be all right. It was springtime in 1911 when the moving began. The box car at the railway spur was packed with all of their household furniture and other belongings. Into another car went all of Axel and Nora Hansen's property and the doors were closed. Both families went directly to the depot and boarded the passenger train. Looking out of the coach windows, they watched the last buildings of Hibbing recede into the distance. Then there were a few farms and finally a wilderness of trees and swampland. It was necessary to change trains at Alborn to get on the Duluth, Mesabi, and Iron Range branch line. A half hour later the conductor came down the aisle calling, "Meadowlands next stop." Gathering their baggage, Lydia and Nora craned their necks looking out the windows to see what manner of place they were approaching. The train came to a halt, and they descended in front of the small depot. There were no other arrivals except the Palmers and the Hansens. The train pulled out, and everyone looked southward. What went through their minds as they gazed at the store, the two-story house, and the small school farther in the distance, is not recorded.

CHAPTER VIII

Meadowlands

The year of 1911 passed swiftly. Charlie and his family occupied the first floor of the only house on the townsite, while Axel and Nora Hansen lived upstairs. Lydia loved to cook and bake while Nora hated both of these chores. She wanted to be a clerk in the store, so an arrangement was made for Lydia to make the meals for both families. She soon found herself loaded with a staggering amount of work, feeding everyone while at the same time doing the washing and ironing for her family and keeping the house clean. In addition, visitors or salesmen arriving by train were always invited in for a meal.

Meanwhile in the store, Charlie, Axel, and Nora Hansen had little to occupy their time. There was no great rush of customers to buy their wares. One person could have easily handled the trade. The store was stocked with everything from meats to clothing, lumber to machinery, to salt herring, but it wasn't moving fast enough. A team of horses and wagon were purchased for making large deliveries such as lumber, but Charlie often found himself spending a whole afternoon driving miles out into the country to deliver a sack of flour. Axel Hansen began to worry. It seemed that there were just not enough people in the area to support a store. Bachelors living out in the woods would come to town and buy flour, salt, herring, tobacco, and matches. Then they would not be seen again for about three months. Periodically, H. C. Hansen would ride down in the Packard to inspect his farm and the store. After dinner he would always leave two dollars by his plate for Lydia before lighting his big meerschaum pipe and rising to go out and discuss business affairs with Charlie and Axel Hansen.

They all hoped that new settlers would bring an increase of business at the store. H. C. had purchased a herd of twenty-five holstein cows for his farm, a team of horses, and a complete outfit of farm machinery. Mr. Albertson was starting off with industry and efficiency. The prospect for success there looked good. H. C. ordered a better well dug at the farmhouse and another one far out in the pasture. Both wells were equipped with windmills and tanks.

There was a good well behind the Palmer-Hansen home. A large pressure tank was buried in the ground, and at the end a hole was excavated to receive pipes beneath the frost line. The hole was about ten feet deep, and there was about a foot of water at the bottom. Axel Palmer brought Victor over to show him the water. Then he got behind Victor, and pushed him into the hole. Victor got up out of the water and his screams brought the womenfolk running from the house. A ladder was lowered into the hole, and he was soon brought to the surface, dried, and changed to clean clothing. Before long a windmill was installed at this well also, the lower part being enclosed with a pumphouse for a gasoline engine to provide water pressure when the winds failed.

Hidden from the townsite by forests, there were more settlers in the area than appearances indicated. A few miles to the northwest Dan Anderson was blasting out a farmstead by the Whiteface River. Closer to the townsite lived the Larson Family, across the road from the Eppards who later sold to the Jochs. Eastward lived the Nelsons, the Andersons, and farther out Big Gus Anderson, no relation, and the Ahlenius family. Mr. Ahlenius alternated between trapping in season, and doing carpentry jobs. To the south old Man Joachim lived with his wife and children, on a high bluff overlooking the Whiteface River. The last four mentioned and Dan Anderson comprised the original group of Swedes who had come by canoe up the St. Louis and Whiteface Rivers to select homesteads. Further south by Spider Creek lived Charlie Swanson, a trapper, his housekeeper Mrs. McCarthy and her two daughters, Elizabeth and Mary. Her son Jack, the oldest of her children, was the depot agent at Meadowlands. Three miles west beyond the St. Louis River, a colony of Germans sponsored by the Catholic Diocese were busy getting settled and clearing the good soil for planting. Northwestward lived the Landgrens, a large family, and to the north, Ellis Speece; his sons and daughters were developing two farms in a partnership later to be known as "Speeceville." Closer to town the Max Schleinitz family moved on to a twenty acre farm by the railroad tracks. Max was a painter by trade, but he had contracted what was known as "painter's disease" in his lungs and had been advised to seek other employment out in the open air, or at least, to paint only out doors.

Across the tracks from the Schleinitzes lived Mr. Albertson with his family on the H. C. Hansen farm. Not to be overlooked was a bachelor, Mr. Shmiedel who lived two miles southwest of Meadowlands. He raised the finest celery on peat lands, hilling the plants as they grew so that only the leaves were above ground. These stalks of his celery were white, crisp, and tender. The excellence of his methods have been long lost in a world of increasing commercialism. But he soon took the zither that he loved to play and moved on to parts unknown.

As a result of the railroad advertising department's campaign, settlers began to arrive in increasing numbers. Some new arrivals lived in the tenement house for a few months while building living quarters on their newly purchased farmsteads. The Methodist Mission completed a church on the townsite. Soon a big nine-room school stood opposite and across the road from the little one-room school.

Charlie Palmer and Axel Hansen were concerned for the effect on their business when Mrs. Ford erected a large store fronting the railroad tracks and installed a barber shop in one end of the building. Farther down the track frontage, Jack O'Brien opened a butcher shop. Next door, "Mac" McCrae started a blacksmith shop where he kept busy shoeing horses. Next in line to open was a hotel. Farmers were planning to erect a creamery northward across the tracks. Gradually the townsite was changing into a small village.

The team of horses that Charlie Palmer and Axel Hansen had purchased were an ill assorted pair. Maude, the mare, was a plodding, even-gated animal. But King, the other half of the team, was a retired firehorse from Hibbing. When a driver said "Giddap," he would start out at full speed, and at the command "Whoa," he would dig his hooves in and stop almost instantaneously. So they were used separately in one horse shafts mounted to the wagon.

One day Charlie had to deliver some supplies to the new school, so he hitched King to the wagon and loaded his children in the wagon also, for a ride. He stopped the wagon at the schoolhouse door, took the box of supplies and entered the building leaving Lillian, Axel, and Victor in the wagon. He didn't know that there were some workmen blasting stumps behind the building. A charge of dynamite detonated while he was inside, and the noise scared King. He took off at top speed heading toward town. Victor was the first to fall out of the wagon. A block farther, one of the wagon wheels struck a rut in the road, and the wagon careened, sending Axel flying over the side. When the horse in full flight turned right, at the first corner, the wagon box flew off with Lillian in it. When King finally stopped running and came to a halt at the depot, only the front wheels of the wagon were left attached to the harness.

Soon, neighbors came to the Palmer home carrying the three children, bruised and bloody. Doctor Sequin was summoned by telegraph, and he came from Bovey on the next train. The children were all in shock, but happily there were no bones broken, and they recovered rapidly.

The writer offers his apologies for having to end the first book of this series with the depressing account of the runaway. But there are compelling reasons why this should be done. First, events chronicled so far happened before and up to the time at which the writer was two and one-half years of age. He had no memory of any of them. They are the distillation of actual accounts of what happened, told by relatives and friends, often piecemeal at times, which stuck in the writer's memory. There has been no attempt at embellishment. At rare intervals it has been necessary to eliminate gaps in the story by indicating what must have happened, or to reconstruct what people said or must have thought as they make their moves and carried on with their daily lives. In a sense, they are the authors of the first book. The writer, Charles Victor, wrote about what he was told.

At the age of three a new faculty was born in me. I began to remember. The world about me became my world, and this is the way it was.

BOOK II

CHAPTER I

Remembrance

To begin with there were only flashes of remembrance, filling the kitchen stove with wood and the reservoir with water, cooking, washing, kerosene lamps being lighted and long hours sitting in the high chair. MY mother Lydia felt sorry for me puffing and sighing, there but she rushed about with too much work to be done, and she was again pregnant. Soon I was released from my high-chair prison.

Events came into focus clearly when I was three years and twenty-three days old. The lamp on its swinging arm on the north wall of our kitchen was lighted, and two straight chairs were placed against the wall beneath it. My brother Axel and I were given orders to sit and stay in the two chairs. Several neighbor ladies hustled about. There was something going on in our parents' bedroom.

As daylight waned, the kerosene lamp cast a dim light over all. No one seemed to be preparing supper. Axel and I sat and waited for several hours. At length one of the ladies rushed by us carrying a bundle in her arms. She went out on the back porch and we heard a couple of slaps followed by small outraged cries of pain. The lady with the bundle hurried past us toward the bedroom again smiling as she went. Then things seemed to settle down again. We were allowed to leave our chairs and were told that we had a new baby brother, Arthur Donald. Once a month, Dr. Sequin arrived by train to examine new babies and make out birth and death certificates for the new arrivals and the departed. Then he caught the evening train back to Bovay.

That summer a vegetable garden was planted in the back yard, and a small room was partitioned off in the wood shed for a Jersey cow. She was usually staked out with a chain in the daytime to forage on the grass behind the woodshed. One day at milking time, my father Charlie went to fetch her, found the stake pulled out and the cow nowhere in sight. The reason for her departure was obvious. A bear was roving about searching for tasty shoots and berries.

Time passed swiftly, and Donald was soon able to toddle about the yard. Charlie had acquired a pair of turkeys, a hen and a gobbler. They soon got out of their enclosure and roamed about the place. One day I stood and watched Donald trudging northward toward the store. He had gotten halfway when the turkey gobbler took wing and flew directly after him. The turkey tried to land upon little brother's head, knocking him down. The bird turned a summersault on the ground, picked himself up, and stalked majestically away.

Axel and Nora Hansen soon had their big two-story home completed across the road from ours and moved out, leaving our upstairs vacant.

That summer Charlie Swanson, the trapper gathered up his traps and drove to town leaving his housekeeper, Mrs. McCarthy and her daughter Mary, at the trapping cabin seven miles south by Spider Creek. Before boarding the train, he asked Charlie Palmer to return the small Horse, "Fly," and the buggy to Mrs. McCarthy, to bring her a sack of flour, and to bring her daughter Elizabeth back to the cabin. When Charlie reached Spider Creek, he realized that Fly would never be able to pull the buggy, loaded as it was, through the deep rushing waters. Stopping at the stream bank, he lifted the sack of flour onto his back, told Elizabeth to climb on the sack, and waded the stream. Then he waded back and led Fly with the empty buggy across to the other side. Loaded again, they proceeded on to the trapper's cabin. Charlie Swanson never returned, and before long Mrs. McCarthy moved into Meadowlands to run the new hotel beside the railroad line. That summer Jack O'Brian abandoned hope that a meat market would flourish in the community and returned to Turtle Lake, Wisconsin.

Lillian Palmer soon became fast friends with Elizabeth and Mary McCarthy. In their sorties around the town site, they learned that Mr. and Mrs. Edgar Speece lived a short way to the west, with their four daughters Edda, Joyce, Thelma, and Wilma. School opened in the fall with the girls enrolled in classes taught by Miss Brecker, still in the little one room schoolhouse. The big new school building was soon opened. With the increasing influx of settlers, it began to fill up rapidly, as large families enrolled their children. Bus routes were established using Conestoga wagons with tops made of canvas stretched over u-shaped uprights. The buses were transferred to sleighs for driving in the winter snow.

The Christ Nelsons moved onto a tract near "Speeceville," soon to be followed by the John Murkers, and Ervin Sausmans who settled north of Landgren's farm. East of town, came the Brittons and, further out, the Nate Sanders and Douglas Felknors to occupy the land. Even further eastward, the John Andersons, the Olson brothers, and the Gustafsons. To the south were the Kupkas and the August Olsons. To the far southwest settled the Dasalles and "Dutch" Sisler, also the Neimans and the McCoys, by the St. Louis River.

Across the St. Louis River, settled the German community: The Grietens, Landauers, Reichs, Warlichs, Horvaths, Novaks, and the Rinqhofers. To the north about twelve miles, a community of Finns began to carve out farms from the forest.

Lands homesteaded or purchased on time payments by all of the settlers ranged in size from eighty to one hundred and sixty acres, much of it wooded. They were of a size on which one man, with the help of his growing family, a team of horses, and a few farm implements, could make a living, if there was a market for his crops. The settlers of this period speedily became almost totally self-sustaining. They raised small herds of cattle, some hogs, chickens, geese, and occasionally, a few sheep. Items purchased at the country stores were confined largely to flour, square, spices, and clothing. One day the Sheriff of St. Louis County stepped from the passenger train and walked over to the

Hansen and Palmer store. He asked Charlie, my father, if he would act as a special deputy sheriff for the area, a job that was only on an "as needed" basis with a small fee while on duty. Charlie agreed to take on the assignment and was given a deputy sheriff's badge. Settlers in the area were peaceful and he was seldom called upon to exercise the responsibilities of a deputy sheriff.

That winter on a cold day in January, the telegraph key in the depot began to chatter, and Jack McCarthy took the message. It was for Charlie, so Jack brought the telegram over to the store. The sheriff's office relayed the information that a bachelor was frozen to death in the snow, close to his shack near Payne, about seven miles east of Meadowlands. It was requested that Charlie drive out, get the body, and ship it to Duluth on the train.

He waited until after supper, then hitched the horse to the wagon, and started out. It was a moonlit night and with the moon reflecting off the snow, he could see quite well. Arriving at the bachelor's cabin, he found that the man had collapsed and frozen in the clearing not far from his home. The arms and hands lay extended out in front of the body and the knees were drawn partly upward.

The rough box that Charlie had brought along to receive the body was in the wagon, so he lifted the frozen corpse out of the snow, carried it to the wagon, and placed him in the box. However, due to the position of the knees and the hand, he was unable to put the cover on the coffin. Charlie got back to Meadowlands about ten o'clock, summoned Jack McCarthy from his house, and they proceeded to the depot to place the body in the "cool" room. When they got the box into the freight room, Charlie decided on another attempt at getting the body into the box with the lid on. He placed the corpse on the floor, face up, and began to push down hard, on the frozen knees. Jack stood by, kerosene lantern in hand, and watched his efforts. Suddenly, the knees gave way, but the rest of the body remained rigid. The hands came up as if to grab Charlie. Jack became so startled that he jumped backward and let out a yell. They finally got the lid on the box and set it into the cool room, ready for shipment the following day.

Bachelors living in lonely cabins back in the woods occasionally became eccentric or what was referred to as "woods happy." One of them began to act queerly and began to carry his rifle about with him. Charlie was notified. He found the man sitting on a stump holding his rifle in readiness. Charlie was unarmed, and he talked with the man for a while, finally persuading him to give up his gun and come into town, whence he was sent to Duluth for examination. Suicide took a heavy toll among these woodsmen. One put the barrel of his shotgun into his mouth and pulled the trigger with his toe. Another used the simple method of tying a rope from the head frame of his bed to the foot frame and laying down with his throat across the rope.

We became so accustomed to the noise of ore trains passing through on the railway that we seldom heard their roar, even at night. Only a change in the pattern of their noise would awaken us, such as when they stopped for water at the tank by the Whiteface river. Even we would recognize the four short toots, "Flag Man Come Back," before they started out again. One night the whistling continued, and people in their beds recognized that it must be some kind of distress call. They dressed hurriedly and went toward the track to determine the cause of the disturbance. While the train had stood still on the tracks taking on water, a bachelor had laid his head on one rail and his feet across the other. Apparently his clothing had caught on the undercarriage because parts of his body were strewn for some distance along the track. The remains were gathered into a basket. Mr. Chapman, superintendent of the school, was there to help with the gathering, but occasionally he would be found down in the ditch retching and vomiting.

A new wave of families arrived: the Espins, the Andrews, Wylies, Chases, Tidds, Huffmans, and the Muellers. Guy Russell came alone from Indiana. Mike Dier, the boss of the railroad section repair gang, moved into the section house at the Whiteface River. There were also a few Czechoslovak families settling on farms to the southwest.

War had broken out in Europe. We heard rumors of large

scale killing and devastation. It wasn't called a World War, and we, of course, would never get into it anyway, we thought. When I was five years old, my mother took me by the hand and led me to school. We found the first grade room, my mother knocked, and Miss Hegler, the teacher opened the door. It seemed we were a bit late, as the desk chairs were already filled with children. But there was a vacant one for me and I was soon in place, ready for instruction to begin. Before long I needed to go to the bathroom so I started squirming in my seat. Miss Hegler divined my predicament and had one of the boys take me to the boy's toilet. When we returned, she explained the signals we were to use if we had to leave the room; the hand raised with one finger extended if you had to urinate, two fingers if you needed to have a bowel movement. The same signals were used all through the grades. Why the teachers had to find out this momentous bit of information, I was I was never able to ascertain. In those days of absolute authority, children were not allowed to ask why.

By the time I started in the second grade, enrollment had increased to such a degree, that the second and third grades were shifted back across the road into the little one room school. We liked it much better there than in the big new building.

Occasionally, during the one hour noon intermission, we were subjected to raids by the older boys from the big school. One day they came armed with bows and arrows and shot holes in the canvas tops of the Conestoga wagons parked in the school yard. When the snow began to melt on the roof of our school building, we invented a new game. You made two snowballs. Then you threw one of them high up on the roof. As it rolled back down, it gathered snow until it was quite large. When it rolled off the roof, the idea was to hit it with the other snowball before it hit the ground. There were no windows on that side of the building. I decided to try the game on the other side, to the south, forgetting for the moment that there were windows all along that side. Up went my first snowball, and it came rolling back down, gathering snow. I threw my second snowball at it as hard as I could. As soon as I let go of the second snowball, I realized that it was travelling straight at a window. Luck was with me that day. The two snowballs collided and exploded, falling harmlessly to the ground. Quaking with relief, I ended my game as the bell called us back to class.

Our time in the second and third grades ended all too quickly, and we were shifted back to the big school across the road to the fourth grade room.

In 1916, with the burgeoning population, a feeling of community began to emerge in the area. The inhabitants wanted to socialize, to do something together. It was decided to have an entertainment evening in the vacant second story above the Hansen and Palmer store. There was a large gathering from town and countryside to watch this first effort at amateur entertainment.

Mrs. Christ Nelson rendered several selections on the piano. Then she accompanied, while Mrs. Max Schleinitz sang "Silver Threads among the Gold," and "Mother." Lorraine Larson was next on the program, singing "I Don't Want to Play in Your Yard, If You Won't Be Good to Me." Several other items followed, and everyone went home with a sense of having seen something that was new and good.

That summer, signs announced that a show was coming from out of town, to take place in a small hall across the road from the Hansen and Palmer store. At show time the little hall was filled with people waiting for the performance to begin. The players were a man, his wife, and their two children, a boy and a girl. The show consisted of two acts. What the acts contained has long since been forgotten. Of more lasting interest was the sales pitch put on between the first and second acts. The father lugged a large box to the stage and extracted from it a bunch of tiny white boxes filled with powdered chalk. He extolled the virtues of the white powder for cleaning teeth to prevent tooth decay and cavities. As he continued his sales talk, mothers in the audience began to doubt the merits of using baking soda as they did at home, when and if it occurred to brush their own and their children's teeth. Elbows poked husbands in the side. For the price of a quarter, many boxes of this wonderful dentifrice were distributed. The men, who ordinarily depended on a pinch of snuff, or a wad of tobacco to prevent tooth decay were not as impressed as the women, but a few of them even bought some for their own use. Next the actor brought another box onto the stage, opened it, and took out some bottles containing a thick red liquid. He instructed the audience that most human ailments were caused by nothing more or less than impure blood. He held in his hands a remedy for this condition called Keystone Blood Purifier. Anyone who took one teaspoonful of this remedy would soon recover and be a healthy person again, and for only fifty cents a bottle. Ailments, real or imagined, began to sprout in the minds of some of the listeners. Sales for this elixir were not, however, as brisk as for the tooth powder. Many felt as though their blood was pure enough already.

Finally, the actor informed his listeners that he was a dentist, that he would be staying at this very hall for a week to take care of any dental repairs needed in the community.

There I sat in the audience with two cavities in my teeth. Nothing could be done to escape it. The next day my mother sent me to get them repaired. The actor, now dentist, sat me down in an improvised dentist's chair. He first showed me a cigar box full of teeth that he had extracted in his travels. They looked polished and white but for a few to which traces of blood and flesh adhered, which made me sink farther into the chair.

Then, pumping a pedal with his right foot, he shoved the drill into on of the cavities, gouged it clean, and then the other one. He filled the cavities with some white stuff called enamel, and I was free.

It was summer and the weather was beautiful. Baby Margret Schleinitz was having her nap in the crib. Carl, Henry, and Fritz were playing out in the farmyard, so Mrs. Schleinitz decided to have a quick visit with Lydia Palmer in town. The walk took her only ten minutes. They were sitting by the table in the Palmer's kitchen exchanging news of the day when someone outside began shouting something about fire. Martha and Lydia hurried out of the kitchen. The men were pointing northwestward and beginning to run in that direction. The Schleinitz's house was burning! Mrs.

Schleinitz ran as fast as she could along with the others, but by the time they reached the house, it was enveloped in flames. Efforts to get to the bedroom to save Margaret were made, but the men were driven back by the extreme heat. The baby died in the fire, and the home was completely destroyed. The Schleinitz family were left only with the clothes on their backs, saddened by the loss of their little girl. A new house was erected upon the site of the old home. The Schleinitz's dug in and held on, striving once more for a successful life on their farm.

Later in the summer of 1916, we Palmers waited in anticipation, for the arrival of Aunt Ida, who was coming on the passenger train from Virginia, Minnesota. We were all at the depot meet her. Beside her suitcases, she had a rectangular box with a round top from which a handle protruded. There was also a long tin horn that went with the box, but that was not as yet fastened to it, and another box. She said that the outfit was an Edison Phonograph.

When we reached home, we placed the phonograph on a table on the front porch, attached the horn by means of some rods provided for that purpose, and slipped one of the cylinder records into place. We wound the machine up with a crank and placed the diamond-needled gadget on the record. Then we stood listening with wonder at the sounds coming out of the shiny horn. There were about twenty records and the playing continued until all were heard, from " Love a Lassie" by Harry Lauder to numbers by Caruso and Sousa, ending finally with some comical songs. I seemed to have the best luck operating the phonograph, so I was chosen to be its operator, that is until we finally got tired of listening, and went on to other amusements.

Deer hunting season opened late in the fall. My father Charlie would take the day off from his duties at the store, hitch the horses to the sleigh, and go off eastward following the trail toward Payne. He invariably arrived home about dark with a nice deer loaded in the wagon box. Sometimes the deer was frozen solid, leading us to wonder if one of Charlie's Svenska friends had helped the hunting along by hanginq a choice buck back among the cedar trees in advance. Whether this happened or not he would never admit.

One deer hunting season, Charlie, Axel Hansen, Frank Zanker, Ray Sanders, Neil McCrae, and several other fellows decided to go hunting in a group down at the now abandoned cabin of trapper Charlie Swanson. They loaded groceries into the new Vim truck borrowed from the H. C. Hansen farm and drove as far as Spider Creek. From there they had to hike as the truck could not be driven across the creek. Forming a line, they trudged along through the snow, becoming a bit careless with their rifles. None of them had much experience with deer hunting. Unexpectedly one of the rifles discharged. The bullet tore a neat hole through the shoe heel of the man in front of the gun. Luckily, the heel itself was not injured. But from that time, carefulness became the word among the hunters.

Charlie shot a rabbit, then another, and had to listen to the jibes of his fellow hunters over fooling with such small game. After all they would soon have deer meat to eat for their supper. Reaching the cabin, he cleaned and sectioned the rabbits. After breakfast the next morning, he prepared a large stew of vegetables and rabbit meat; this was to cook on a slow fire in the kitchen stove while the gang went out to hunt deer. They hunted all day, returning empty-handed and exhausted, to dig into Charlie's rabbit stew with relish, calling it the best stew they had ever had.

Charlie loved to tell a story which probably originated back in the early days of logging in Wisconsin, about the group of loggers who had no cook for their camp. Finally one of the group decided to take over the cooking duties on one condition. Anyone who complained about the food he prepared would have to take over the cook's job. The others agreed to this arrangement, and the reluctant cook worked away at his post for several weeks, growing more weary of it day by day. Finally he prepared a large kettle of vegetable beef stew and poured about a pound of salt into it. When the loggers returned to camp that evening, each of them ladled out a large bowl of the stew and started to eat.

One of them tasted his soup and exclaimed, "Jesus, this stew is sure salty' But he quickly added, "That's just the way I like it."

The story does not go on to tell whether he became the new cook. Charlie told that story to so many people that eventually they believed that he was the man in the tale who said, "Jesus, this stew is salty," though he never logged a day in his life.

As to telling stories, this one was told by Carl Ahlenius, a long-time area lumberman. There was a railroad side track at the southwest edge of Maple Lake in Prosit. It was used for then purpose of loading railroad cars with logs from an adjacent logging camp. The logging boss had a problem each time that payday rolled around. At those times quite a few of his lumberjacks would drift away to the Superior, Wisconsin, brothels and saloons where they would stay until their money ran out. He finally hit upon a solution to this truancy, as it crippled his logging operation severely. At the end of each month, payday was held on Sunday. On that day a railroad car furnished in brothel fashion, complete with women, was shunted onto the siding. Subsequently, there were no more desertions by the crew until the winter's logging was completed.

Charlie, Axel, and I rode westward one day, behind our horse "King" hitched to the wagon. We turned southward after passing the Edgar Speece home and drove a short distance when another horse and wagon pulled up beside us going toward town. As was the custom, father stopped to exchange greetings and pleasantries. It happened that the other driver was Lewis Miller. Axel and I had never seen him before. He stuttered. No, to say that is not enough. He stuttered beyond all stuttering. First he screwed up his mouth but no sound came out. This was followed by some grimacing, and gradually the sounds, "Haw. Haw. Haw." broke the silence. Finally, the words began to come, interspersed with all manner of facial contortions. Axel and I had never witnessed a performance such as this before. We looked at each other and started giggling, though we tried to hold it back. We were only six and eight years old at the time. Later acquaintance with Lewis Miller would prove him to be one of the finest men in our township. Once we got used to his speech impediment, we hardly noticed it. He was a hard worker and a jolly fellow.

One fine summer evening, our father and mother put us to bed and went to a party at Furiel's Lodge by the Whiteface River. We were left alone with the windows open and the doors unlocked. Nobody ever locked doors at that time in Meadowlands. Keys were used so seldom that they were often lost or hard to find. Lillian, Axel, and Donald were soon asleep, but I lay tossing and turning, thinking about the party. I became aware of a slight rustling and rasping noise in front of the house, and raising myself on one elbow, I looked out the window. I could just barely discern the outline of a form in the darkness standing within the fence gateway. It had two long legs, a short body with a long neck, and a long narrow head. It was like nothing human. It just stood there in the gateway facing directly at the house. I lay back in the bed terrified, threw the covers over my head, and listened to the beating of my heart. For some time I lay there, wishing my father and mother were home. After what seemed an interminable length of time, I summoned up enough courage to venture another look. The monster was still there, doing nothing as before. I decided to watch it. Gradually, it began to move backwards out of the gate, and when it turned sideways, I could perceive the dim out line of a horse. Someone's horse had gotten loose and was roaming about. I flopped back into bed and was asleep almost instantly.

One day Jack McCarthy came over to the store, and he had a problem. Several months previously a nursery salesman had been through the area taking orders for fruit trees and berry bushes. He had sold a large order to one man who, now that the merchandise had arrived, could not be found. The nursery instructed Jack to sell the order for whatever he could get and remit the money to them. Charlie knew nothing about fruit trees or berry bushes, but he was fond of fruit, so he bought the lot for twenty-five dollars. Soon we had four crab apple trees planted across the front yard, compass cherry trees beside them near the fence, and several varieties of plums both north and south of our home. Then there was a whole row of current bushes by the north fence and even a pear tree by the pump house. Grape vines were planted on the south side of the pump house to take advantage of more continuous sunlight in that location. Surprisingly all of the nursery stock took hold and grew. We waited patiently to see what our orchard would produce, leaving the tags in place so that the varieties could be identified.

Our school was filled to capacity with children. It became necessary to place the rows of seats side by side leaving only one aisle for two desks in order to provide room for more students. The subjects taught were standard for the time: grammar, arithmetic, spelling, history, and geography, with occasionally some penmanship and singing. Many of the songs we sang were of civil war vintage: "Tenting on the Old Camp Ground," "Battle Hymn of the Republic," "Sweet and Low," among others. Most villages still had an old tottering Civil War veteran lingering on.

For each subject we had a study period. It would have been useless for us, especially the boys, to take books home to study, for as soon as we arrived there were chores to be done until suppertime, which was quite late in the evening. The new horse-drawn buses with glass windows were a big improvement over the old canvas tops, but they travelled no faster. It took some students who lived farther out in the country over an hour to reach their homes after school each day. There was no organized physical education program, so for recesses and at noon we made up our own game. It was called "Pump, Pump, Pull Away, If You Don't Come, I'll Pull You Away." There were two goals; one was along the road in front of the school. The other was a strip even with the school building itself. A couple of pupils would be "it," that is they would stand between the two goals. The idea was to run from one goal to the other without getting caught by an "it." Little by little everyone would get caught, and the game would begin all over again.

The young men folk of Meadowlands organized a baseball team. They began to schedule games with close neighboring communities, and people turned out on Sundays to watch them play. Scheduling games was difficult because the roads were poor, and as yet, there were only one or two automobiles in the whole area, none of them owned by baseball players. Occasionally a railway speeder would be "borrowed" for transportation to a game up or down the railroad line.

It happened that one day some of the men of our family and their friends went fishing. They had fabulous luck and brought home many fish, including a northern pike that weighed about twenty pounds. It was decided to have an evening fish dinner at our home. The Schleinitzes, McCarthys, and Hansens were invited for the Sunday evening event, and preparations went into high gear as Mother set about the task of stuffing the large pike for baking, with the smaller fish around the side, all garnished with butter sauce and parsley. It was a regular banquet, with fish for the main attraction.

Meanwhile the baseball players had gone to Silica on the speeder for a Sunday afternoon game of baseball. Jack McCarthy was catcher on the team, and it was thought that he would be back in plenty of time for the dinner. Our guests arrived, all but Jack. His wife May waited at their home for him, but finally she came, bringing their three children. Lydia became worried about the food getting cold so dinner was served. We finished eating, and Jack had still not arrived. Finally the party broke up, and May gathered her children and returned home. During the night word began spreading of a speeder accident somewhere up the line.

The baseball team had started back from Silica about dusk. Meanwhile, two carpenters were travelling northward from Proctor on the same tracks. Neither speeder had lights. In the last moments before they collided, some of the riders became aware of their danger and jumped off. There were many injuries and broken limbs. Jack McCarthy was killed. The town was stricken with grief. May McCarthy and her three children lived on in the Agent's house for several months. Then the family returned to her parents' home in Turtle Lake. The game of baseball winked out in Meadowlands. It was several years before play was resumed.

We had a stove called a baseburner in our living room. It was a beautiful stove all covered with nickel plated parts. It had gargoyles sticking out at the corners and a high ornamental top which shifted to the side for pouring in anthracite coal, the only kind it was designed to burn. There were glass windows in the doors across the middle to show the glowing fire. People often remarked that as they walked by our home, they would look through the front windows and see those glowing coals in the stove, looking so cozy and warm. It was a pretty illusion. The stove gave off only reflective heat. Furthermore, it was supposed to heat not only the living room but two connecting bedrooms as well. During the midwinter months with the temperature twenty or thirty degrees below zero outside, we were forced to keep the bedroom doors closed until about fifteen minutes before bedtime. Then we opened them, hastily undressed, put on our nighties, and climbed into bed. Quilts and blankets formed a cover about four inches thick. It took a lot of shivering and clinging together to warm the beds enough so that we could go to sleep.

At about the age of seven, our working life began, especially the boys. There was wood to be chopped to fill the woodbox, the baseburner had to be filled with coal, and the ash boxes to empty. Cows must be herded to the barn for milking and water pumped for them to drink. All of these and other tasks had to be completed before we went to and after we returned from school every day. With the advent of summer and the growing gardens, we were introduced to that awful tool, the hoe. It wasn't until we attained the ripe age of eight, that we began to take on the tasks of grown men. But there was plenty of time for play too, mostly after supper was eaten and it was dark outside. In winter we would walk to the Whiteface River, fasten skates to our shoes by means of clamps operated with a key, and glide around on the ice close to a bonfire burning on the riverbank. Other nights, in the bright moonlight, we ran down the street and bellyflopped onto our sleds to skim along a few yards. It was great fun. We always worked hard at getting and decorating a tree for Christmas. But at Christmas time in 1916, there seemed to be no talk of presents, so on Christmas Eve I asked mother if we could hang up our stockings for a present. She said that I would be getting a handkerchief. I remember answering, "Ah, Ma!" Later I heard her discussing something with my father; then he left the house.

On Christmas morning I found a six inch long wooden rowboat with a man in it holding onto a pair of oars in my stocking. Never before or since have I cherished a present as much as I did that little boat. I waited long months until spring melted the snow to find a puddle in which to launch it with visions of it skimming through the water propelled by the sailor with his oars. Spring arrived. I put the boat in the water. For some reason it tilted sidewise. When I pushed it, it would only go a few inches. Whatever happened to it after that I do not know.

In 1915 Charlie had begun to realize that he really wasn't cut out to be a storekeeper. His first goal had always been to have a farm of his own. Mr. Agnew had decided to sell his farm located just south of the Meadowlands' townsite, and Charlie's brother Werner wanted to become a partner in the farming enterprise, so they applied to H. C. Hansen for the six thousand and five hundred dollars needed to purchase the farm, signed a mortgage, and thereby became farmers. In the meantime Mr. Albertson who was operating H. C.'s big farm had become discouraged trying to run the place by himself. He decided to move out of the area. H. C. asked Charlie and Werner to run his farm in conjunction with their own, and they agreed. H. C. brought in a new man, Mr. Morgan, to take Charlie's place in the store, so he moved, together with his wife and son, into the vacant upstairs of Charlie's home. Mr. Morgan was an easy-going fellow who liked to spend his free hours playing the guitar. At about the same time Old Fredrick had died in Turtle Lake, so Grandma Sarah, Anna, and Werner were moved to Meadowlands, and into the house on the H. C. Hansen farm. The farm in Turtle Lake was sold to a M. Wagner, later to be purchased by Charlie's brother Axel, when he and Anna Peterson were married. They turned the Turtle Lake acreage into a good productive farm and in time raised three daughters, Eleanor, Muriel, and Joyce.

Lydia, our mother, was a kind, even tempered jolly and hospitable lady, and she loved company. She spoke with a decided Finnish accent. Accents were not uncommon at the time in Meadowlands. In at least half of the families, the parents were of foreign birth. Many of them never did learn to speak English. Rather than Charlie learning Finnish or Lydia learning Swedish,

61

they compromised and both learned to speak English, such as it was, in our home.

After the Axel Hansen's moved across the street to their new home, Lydia's tremendous workload eased somewhat. In contrast to the workload assigned to Axel, me, and later Donald, Lillian did almost nothing. In her later years she often remarked that Lydia never taught her to cook. There is an element of truth in this, but it requires some explanation. When Lillian was assigned to make a cake, she would dally around, waving the mixing spoon, singing songs, and stopping now and then to dip her finger in the batter to taste it. She took so long to complete the task that mother, who was efficiency itself, would run out of patience, tell Lillian to run along, and finish the cake herself. Neighbor ladies would occasionally ask mother why Lillian never did any of the work. Lydia would reply, "Oh, let them have fun while they are young." It was not a good excuse, but it served mother's purpose of not having Lillian underfoot, holding up the work, and it served Lillian as a reason for not having learned to cook.

Lillian, was great friends with Edda and Joyce Speece, and they were full of the dickens. One day they told Lydia that she and Mrs. Max Schleinitz were invited to Mrs. Edgar Speece's house for a party. They delivered the same invitation to Mrs. Schleinitz. At the appointed time Mrs. Schleinitz walked to town, joined Lydia, and they walked together out to the Speece farm. When Mrs. Speece opened the door, she seemed somewhat surprised to see them, but she invited them in. It became apparent that she was in the midst of washing clothes. Nevertheless, she made them feel at home and brought out some leftover pudding and made some coffee, so they had a nice visit. However, they soon realized that the girls had played a joke on them. Strangely enough, they didn't get angry at the girls or scold them when they got home. About a month later, Lillian was walking home from H. C. Hansen's farm where Werner, Anna, and Grandma were living. As she passed the Schleinitz farm, Mrs. Schleinitz called her over and asked if she would carry a bag of farm produce home to Mother. She asked her to carry it very carefully as there were some eggs on top. The bag was very heavy, and Lillian was glad to finish walking the half mile home. She gave the bag to her mother. When they opened the bag, it was found to contain nothing but rocks.

Charlie and Werner plunged into the farming venture with vigor. They soon found that extra help was needed to handle the large acreage and care for the big herd of cows, so they hired a young fellow named Albert Turbutt to assist them. Working the two farms together provided an awkward arrangement. The Palmer acreage lay south of the townsite, whereas the H. C. Hansen acreage was northwest of town. Thus, produce, hay, and equipment had to be hauled a full mile from the Palmer farm to the Hansen farm by team and wagon or hay rack. Then too the road north out of Meadowlands separated the H. C. Hansen pasture from the farm itself on which the house and barn were located. It was necessary to drive the cattle one quarter of a mile twice a day to and from the pasture in summer. Ere long the latter task fell to brother Axel, me, and the dog Shep. We were busier that ever. Soon Axel found other interests, and I had the job alone. In addition, it was found that we could milk the "strippers," cows that were going dry, so that chore was also added.

One day during haying season, I walked to the pasture, gathered the herd, and drove them to the barn. I was eight years old at the time. Soon I had them all in their stanchions and began milking my strippers. I milked five of them and began to worry because no one showed up from the Palmer farm where haying was in progress. So I started out to look for the men and finally met them near the depot, hauling a load of hay. I told my father that I had milked five cows and was worried because they hadn't come to the barn. My father answered, "Why didn't you milk some more?" We learned early that father was not lavish with praise. Nor was he ever demonstrative of his feelings. We, his children, felt that he liked us. But I do not remember any of us receiving a kiss from him. He was, in fact, the father figure for two families, those of his father, and those of his own. We sometimes felt that we rated second to our older relatives.

Aunt Anna soon got a job clerking in the Hansen and Morgan

63

store. Then she changed jobs to become a teller in the new bank across the street. Hers was a cheerful, friendly, outgoing personality, mature and self sufficient. Werner developed well along the same lines, manly, and handsome. Fred, on the other hand, turned out to be irascible, quarrelsome, and opinionated. In winter when the mines closed down, he would make his home with either the Palmers in Meadowlands or in Turtle Lake. Room had to be provided for him even if it meant turning children out of a bedroom to be crowded in with others. He did little to help but was always there at mealtime. When spring came and he was ready to leave for his locomotive running job, he would hand father ten dollars to pay for his winter's keep. It made my mother's blood boil. Fred did not smoke, chew, or drink. His main interest was taking pictures with his excellent Kodak. The Palmers were indebted to him for photographs taken of our daily lives and of memorable events in those early years, if for nothing else. In a sense he never grew up.

Farmers in the area were hard pressed for cash to buy implements to work the land. Almost all of the farming equipment that they were able to afford was second hand. When a machine broke, it was patched up with baling wire and returned to service until it broke down again. Father bought a second hand two-cylinder, Waterloo Boy tractor with enormous cleated wheels on the rear and small wheels on the front. Dan Johnson bought a used Moline tractor which had large wheels in the front and small wheels in the back. Then they went into partnership to purchase a threshing rig, a binder, a side delivery rake, and a dump rake. All second hand, of course. The threshing machine, a Belle City, was of ancient manufacture. Straw was expelled onto an incline and was pushed upwards by a series of slats motivated by chain links at both ends, which formed chains. The straw was dropped off of the end of the incline, to be pushed away by a man with a pitch fork. This required two men if the straw pile became large. To feed the machine, two men were required, one to cut the twine bands, the other to throw the bundles into the rig. Two more men were needed to sack the grain which ran out of a pipe at the side.

There were usually three teamsters with teams and hayracks to bring bundles in from the fields and three bundle pitchers to toss bundles up to the teamsters.

In all about twelve men were required to thresh grain, not counting the water boy. They moved from farm to farm exchanging work for work, to avoid hiring labor. Grain produced from the virgin soil in those first years was fabulous, especially on the townsite where it grew to a height above our shoulders.

The St. Louis County roads department had surveyed, graded, and gravelled the narrow roads, so travel was made easier in the district except in spring when large mud holes appeared. Teams with wagons sometimes got stuck on Main Street. School buses were drawn by farm horses not noted for their speed. One driver, Pete Mitchum, had a horse that would lie down in his stall at night, so Pete had to rig a hoist to raise him up every morning before starting on the bus route.

Henry Schleinitz reported that an automobile had been brought in on a railroad flat car. Then one day I happened to be looking out of the kitchen window northward toward the store. I saw what appeared to be a buggy drive in and park. But there was no horse in front to pull it. I went over to investigate. There was no shaft for a horse attached to the front. But there was a small, one cylinder engine in the rear behind the seat. Instead of reins to guide the horse ! there was a bar protruding from the floor, which bent at right angles above the seat. After looking this strange contraption over, I went back to the house and never saw it again. With the improving roads, more automobiles, mostly second hand, began to appear, chugging over the gravel. Frank Zanker bought a big, old Mitchell; Uncle Werner bought a second hand Chevrolet touring car, and Nate Sanders acquired a model T Ford with the back seat cut off and replaced with a box for use as a small truck. They painted the whole vehicle green, so it became known as the June Bug. Meanwhile, the Palmers still depended on the old Vim truck with its acetylene lights to haul cream to the depot for shipment to Duluth. People continued to come in and settle. People with names like Thompson, Yock, Eischen, and Fegreus.

Mr. Froelich, an itinerant peddler bought Mrs. Ford out and took over the store by the railroad tracks. Farm production increased tremendously, but prices for farm products, grain, and cream were low. Farmers were barely squeaking by.

Mr. Morgan, who had replaced Charlie as partner in the store, became discouraged and moved with his family from the community. H. C. Hansen, who had sunk a lot of his money into the store, his farm, and lots on the townsite became disillusioned with his Meadowlands ventures. He decided to move Axel Hansen, his nephew, back to Hibbing and dispose of his holdings. The store was sold to the Max Schlinitz's and the big farm to Peter Roth. H. C. retained but a few lots on the townsite.

Across from the Sampson farm stood a bungalow formerly owned by Mr. Inman, who had moved away. It was purchased by Werner Palmer, who moved it beside Charlie's home. Werner, Anna, and Grandma Sarah were soon moved into the new location. The farming situation proved easier and more efficient now that Charlie and Werner could concentrate work on their own farm. Werner bought a Fordson tractor and was kept busy farming the east forty acres, while Charlie worked the west forty, leaving the south forty in forest.

The war dragged on in Europe, developing into a stalemate, the soldiers living winter and summer in trenches. There were efforts by many in the East to drag the United States into the war. Voters objected, voicing their sentiments in no uncertain terms by electing Woodrow Wilson President because he promised to keep us out of the European Conflict. But munitions manufacturers were shipping boatloads of guns and ammunition to England and France. Finally, the Kaiser declared that furnishing the Allies with war equipment was an act of war, that ships carrying arms would be sunk by the German submarine force. Little of this controversy was carried in the newspapers. People were largely ignorant of the whole situation. Then the newspapers, in large headlines, brought news that the ship, Lusitania, had been torpedoed and sunk by German submarines, that it had gone down in the sea with a large number of passengers, many of them Americans. A wavy of fury and indignation swept the country. Faced with the people's wrath, Congress and the President declared war on Germany. The newspapers did not mention the fact, and it would not be admitted until forty years later, that the Lusitania was also loaded with munitions for France and England. President Wilson's pledge had failed.

The nation was swept with a wave of patriotic fervor. We were going over there and whip the Kaiser! It was going to be a war to end all wars. Armaments must be manufactured and men trained for this great effort. All differences were forgotten in one common purpose. We plunged forward with our preparations for war. There were guns to be forged, song s to be composed, and food to he grown. Few people stopped to wonder how we had gotten ourselves involved.

Mr. Lemieux moved into the upstairs portion of our home. His job was to guard the railroad bridges from saboteurs who might try to blow them up and interrupt the steady flow of iron ore needed to make tanks, ships, and guns for our armed forces. Evenings he would teach young men of the town all of the skills of soldiers on the march. We young boys would find a stick or a broom handle and fall in behind the men marching around the hall. Our efforts usually ended in a shambles, to the amusement of the grownups.

One hot summer evening our menfolk decided to walk over to Ford's store for a bottle of beer. Brother Axel and I had worked beside them all day, so they invited us to come along for a bottle of pop. The beverages purchased, we went out of the store on the shady side toward the tracks and sat on some beer boxes to enjoy our drink.

Suddenly, a Model T touring car with its top down came around the corner, turned and backed up to where we sat. The driver, dressed in a black swallowtail coat and a black bowler hat on his head, stepped into the back seat of the car and proceeded to give us a five minute lecture on the "Evils of strong drink," while we listened open-mouthed. His lecture finished, the stranger went around to the front of his car, turned the crank, remounted, and shot back around the corner again. Calmly, we finished our assorted drinks and returned home. That was the beginning of a new crusade later to be named the "Good Temperance League." Soon meetings were called to exhort the people against the use of alcoholic beverages, to sign up, join the League, and "take the pledge." The Meadowlands meeting was well attended and was considered a success. It was decided to have another meeting to promote the cause at Alborn, fourteen miles to the southeast on the following week. Among the pledgers was a Swede bachelor, a slow talking, somewhat comic character. Carried along by the fervid arguments, he duly signed his card to abstain from alcoholic beverages. The meeting at Alborn was held on schedule. But somewhere on the trip there the bachelor was somehow delayed. One thing led to another, and he had, as the saying goes, "fallen off the wagon." When he arrived, the meeting was in full progress. In he came, staggering and roaring his way down the aisle. The record does not indicate whether he broke up the meeting or he served as an example for all to behold.

Whether by enlistment, or being drafted, young men of Meadowlands were leaving to enter the United States Army. Hired help became scarce, so the work hours increased on farms and businesses. Prices for meat and farm produce began to rise sharply. The farmers were elated. They began to increase production acreage and for the first time since colonization began at Meadowlands, they made good money.

The Cole family, who lived one half mile west of town, moved away, and father bought some of their furniture: a large round oak table with leaves for expansion and six chairs, a rocking chair, a library table, and a davenport which opened to form a bed. We finally stored the old baseburner out in the back shed and replaced it with a circulating stove, a wood burner that gave more heat, so we could be comfortable in winter.

We also changed to new gas mantle lamps, except in our bedrooms. But the old wooden tub washer on legs with the agitator operated by means of a wooden handle sticking up on the side, finally fell apart. Mother was reduced to rubbing clothes on a scrubbing board.

Meanwhile, more automobiles were beginning to appear on the roads about town. The Good Temperance League was in full cry, and Mr. Volstead was urging passage of his law banning the manufacture and sale of alcoholic liquors.

Charlie and Werner plus Axel and I were busy working the farm, but many improvements were needed to bring it into full production, so Charlie temporarily took a job as a night watchman at an iron mine in Aurora, while Werner started an automobile repair business in a warehouse by the railroad; his aspirations toward life as a farmer began to wane. When Charlie returned in the spring and got the crops planted, it looked like we were back to normal again. But he was soon hired by the St. Louis County Highway Department to maintain county roads in the area. Werner's garage business increased so that he had little or no time for farming. The process was gradual, but Axel, Donald, and I eventually found ourselves doing practically all of the farm work, except binding and threshing grain. Axel was twelve years old, I was ten, and Donald was seven. We made no decisions as to running the place. Father would dash out on evenings and Sundays, decide what we should do next, and give us directions. Werner appeared less often at the farm. Charlie soon had us working his portion of the land as well. This while we were going to school nine months of the year. We plowed, disked, seeded, and cultivated crops with the tractor in summer. Mornings and evenings we cared for eight head of cattle and fifteen sheep.

But we received good food, and our home life was enjoyable. At times, our clothing was not adequate for the cold of winter. We had to carry the milk home mornings and evenings during the winter. It wasn't easy to face a north wind at twenty or thirty below with a bucket of milk in each hand. The pail handle would stop the blood circulating to our fingers, and they would begin to freeze. When the fingers would thaw, the pain would be almost unbearable, and we would cry. Finally Mother got after father about it, and we got good leather mittens with wool liners. Father never seemed to think of such matters. One year oats were planted on Werner's forty acres. The seed had not been fanned, and it was full of mustard seed. When the grain came up, there was a heavy stand of mustard flowers turning the whole field yellow. Axel, Donald, and I were sent out to pull the mustard, day after day. In the fall we were given a quarter to go to a show. Axel, Donald, and I often wondered what our efforts were worth, but we never asked and never found out. There was excitement in driving a tractor, driving a team of horses, or helping the ewes at lambing time.

Charlie's church in Berga, Sweden. Completed 1824.

Same Church, interior of sanctuary.

Dedication parchment of congregation dated 1279.

Berga Stadsprivilegier År 1279

Lydia Maki's Church in Ikaalinen, Finland.

Anita Formulati's cabin lakeside, Finland in 1983.

Viola and Charles V. Palmer at above cabin in 1983.

Saloon in
Virginia,
Minnesota
about 1900.
Charles
Fredrick

Lydia's brother, Frank Maki, and her sister, Ida Maki, 1911.

From left to right: Lillian, Charles V., and Axel Palmer, about 1911.

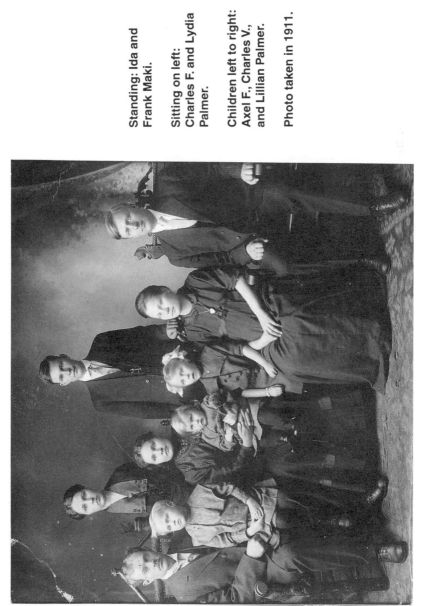

Standing: Ida and
Frank Maki.

Sitting on left:
Charles F. and Lydia
Palmer.

Children left to right:
Axel F., Charles V.,
and Lillian Palmer.

Photo taken in 1911.

Lower left:
Fredrick
and Sarah
Palm.
Upper right:
Fred and
Anna Palm,
1912.

Arriving at
the farm in
Turtle Lake,
Wisconsin,
1910.

Turtle Lake,
Wisconsin
in 1910.

Barn on H. C. Hansen's farm in Meadowlands.

Meadowlands in 1914. Axel, Vic and Donald pictured on left.

New school in Meadowlands, 1916.

Land office in Meadowlands, 1912.

D.I.R. RY. Co. LAND OFFICE, MEADOWLANDS, MINN.

Meadowlands' Fourth of July celebration, 1915.

Palmer Home in Meadowlands, about 1917.

Waiting for the train in the depot in Meadowlands, 1915.

Farmhouse on H. C. Hansen's farm. Pictured: Grandma Sarah, Anna Laura Arnebeck, and Charles F. Palmer.

Palmer family, 1926.

Lillian, Axel, Charles VIctor, and Donald in 1915.

Binding grain. Charles V. Palmer, second from left.

Cutting seed potatoes, 1922.

The mighty hunters, 1914.

Building a kid's cabin in the woods in 1922.

Charles Victor Palmer, 1927.

Meadowlands, 1930. The school is the large building on right.

Charles F. Palmer home, 1930.

Charles "Vic" Palmer. Graduation from
Hibbing Junior College, 1929.

Vic Palmer,
1933.

Vic Palmer,
1944.

U.S. Army Air Corps,
1944.

Charles V. Palmer
home in Duluth,
1958.

Larry and "Marg" Paulson
(Vic's sister).

Viola Tormondsen Palmer,
1938.

Palmer family,
1955: Charles
"Vic" Palmer,
Viola, Pauline,
and Sandra.

Joel Palmer, B.A. in 1966.

Dr. Sandra Palmer Ramer, M.D., 1975.

Pauline Palmer Cable, M.A., M.L.I.S.

Viola Palmer on Champs Elysee, Paris, 1983.

CHAPTER II

World War I, Temperance, and the "Flu"

In the summer of 1918, news about the war in Europe was optimistic. Gradually, we were driving the Kaiser's forces back. Meantime the temperance movement gained strength throughout the land. We harvested our crops and prepared for school in September. The term began on schedule and continued through October. But by the last week of that month, a lot of people were becoming ill. Within another week, so many children, their parents, and teachers were sick with what was called the "Spanish Influenza," that the schools were closed. The epidemic was severe and devastating. Some teachers left town to wait while it ran its course. Others were too ill to return home and were cared for in their rooming quarters. But some hardy souls decided to go out and care for stricken families. Miss Krueger, a teacher who lived upstairs at our home, was one of these. Each morning, she walked down the tracks to help care for the Mike Dier family. Mike was the railway section boss. When she returned from her duties about four o'clock in the afternoon, Miss Krueger would stop in for coffee and a short visit with Mother before going upstairs to her rooms. Several days later, the Dier's baby died in an unusual manner. Miss Carlson, the Red Cross nurse, took specimens with a swab, sealed it in a test tube, and sent that to Duluth for analysis. There, it was determined that the baby had died of diphtheria. Quickly, the Diers were quarantined, and Miss Krueger was also tested for the disease. Her tests came back negative, so she left for her home in Minneapolis. But since she had visited with us during the time she had worked with the Diers, we were also given the swab tests. Returning test results showed that we too, had been exposed to diphtheria, and we were immediately quarantined. Father's test came back negative, and he was not allowed to come into our house. This was lucky for us because he could continue to provide food, milk, and fuel for us during our incarceration. For us, the quarantine lasted from the first week of November until New Year's Day. I lay in bed on November eleventh and listened to a train locomotive whistle blowing like mad. When father arrived with our food later that day, he told us that the whistle was blowing because the war in Europe was ended. An armistice had been signed. Miss Carlson continued swabbing our throats and sending the tubes to Duluth. It seemed that no sooner than one of us would show a negative culture than another would show positive.

Thanksgiving Day arrived, and it was about eleven-thirty in the morning. Mother was busy at the stove, mashing potatoes and making gravy. The table was all set for dinner in our kitchen. There was a knock at our kitchen door. Lillian opened it, and Axel Hansen, standing about thirty feet away so as not to become infected, shouted that he had left some blackberry cider for us on the step. Lillian thanked him, brought the two quart Mason fruit jar inside, and placed it on the sideboard. She asked Mother if we could have some before dinner. Mother was busy at the stove and couldn't stop, so she said, "Yes, go ahead." I don't really think that with her limited English, she understood what cider was. So Lillian poured out four large water glasses, one for each of us children. Axel and I liked ours, and we proceeded to drink it all down immediately. But when Lillian and Donald tasted theirs , they didn't like it. Axel and I quickly downed their glasses too. In about ten minutes, dinner was placed on the table, and we sat down for our Thanksgiving feast. Axel and I sat side by side. Suddenly, and for no apparent reason, we both stood up and started punching each other as hard as we could in the face, chest, and stomach. Mother told us to stop! She had never seen such conduct before. She looked at us , then at Lillian. They stood watching us for a moment, and finally Mother went over to that

Mason fruit jar, took the lid off, and sniffed. Her suspicions were confirmed. That cider packed a real wallop.

So Mother and Lillian went into the living room, opened up the davenport, and brought out the mattress. Axel and I, aged ten and eight, respectively, staggered out to the davenport and laid down. It was eight o'clock in the evening before we awoke.

By January 1, 1919, the flu epidemic had largely run its course, and the schools reopened. We were elated over the Allied victory in Europe, and a few of our soldiers began to return home. Mr. Volstead and the Temperance League had also won a victory. Alcoholic beverages were prohibited throughout the United States. There was a great crusade of smashing whiskey, wine, and beer bottles throughout the country. After their big victory binge in France, our boys returned home to find no liquor available for another celebration. Quickly, they shed their uniforms and bean to hunt for jobs. Where ever they went, we children followed, admiring our conquerinq heroes. My uncle Andrew, the tailor, did not return home for some time. He had been caught in an attack of poisonous mustard gas and spent many months in a Veteran's hospital before being released. He would never completely recover and was in and out of treatment centers until his death in nineteen twenty-six.

CHAPTER III

The Forest Fires

Nineteen Hundred and Nineteen was the year of the great forest fires. There was little rain that year. Forest areas lay dry as tinder. Frequently, we had strong winds from the south. A fire started below Cloquet and swept northwards, leveling a part of that town. From there it spread westward, eastward, and northward burning thousands of acres of timber. One arm of the fire forged north towards Meadowlands until it reached a large area of cultivated land south of town where it burned itself out. But beneath the surface of the ground, there were many areas where the soil consisted of muskeg or peat. This soil was dry, and it smoldered like tobacco in a pipe for several years, winter and summer. These slow fires threatened to undermine roads built across the bogs. At night, when the wind died down, pockets of fire in the roadsides would send up plumes of smoke, so it was decided to take pumps operated by gasoline engines and extinguish the peat fires during the night. Harold Froelich and I operated one of these pumps. We got our water through a suction hose dropped into a deep ditch. After a while, the engine began to labor hard, and the water dwindled to a mere trickle from the fire hose. We began to wonder what was wrong. At length, we took the head off of the pump and found that the inside was packed with small fish. We cleaned the fish out, replaced the head, and were soon operating again, stopping occasionally to remove more fish.

The winter of nineteen twenty-two was extremely cold. In January, a gale swept in from the northwest, accompanied by a heavy snowfall. Then the wind increased, and the temperature dropped to fifty-two degrees below zero. It was the coldest temperature on record for that region. Snow piled into high drifts so hard that one could walk on them like cement. When the weather moderated, we hollowed the drifts out. They made wonderful igloos.

We sat in school one day when someone came into the room and told us that Froelich's store was on fire. Our teacher allowed us to gather at the windows to watch. There was another of those cold northwest gales at ten below again, whipping the flames. The store was quickly consumed by the fire. It jumped next to some sheds, then to the meat market, and finally to the hotel. By nightfall, all of the buildings standing in a row along the railroad track were in ashes.

We often chuckled about how Charlie, our Father, became an expert at growing fruit. The only thing he really knew about fruit was that he liked to eat it. Everyone knew that fruit trees wouldn't grow as far north as Meadowlands. But the trees that Jack McCarthy urged on Charlie after they were left in the depot unclaimed, flourished and began to bear cherries, plums, and crabapples in great quantity. The currant and raspberry bushes turned out to be heavy producers. True, the crabapples were sour, but they made wonderful pickles and apple butter. The pear tree needed a mate to bear fruit, so no fruit there. The grapevines bore large clusters of grapes, but they never ripened because of early frosts. We soon rooted them out. As fall approached and fruit hung heavy and ripe on the branches, neighbors came to see and taste. The word spread. Soon delegations of farmers from other communities came to see this wonder for themselves. The county agriculture agents brought people to inspect our trees. It was lucky for us that we had left the tags attached to them, so we could tell those who inquired the varieties of trees in our orchard. Nurseries must have been surprised by the large number of orders coming from our area.

On March the seventh of nineteen twenty-two, I came home from school and walked through the kitchen into the living room. Mother called to me and told me to go and look in the basket placed on a bench by the bedroom door. I peered down into the basket and saw a tiny, grave face looking back at me.

"That's your new little sister," Mother explained. I looked again. She was so tiny, clean, and nice. "What's her name?" I asked. "Margaret Cathleen." I accepted her as my sister. She looked okay to me.

The Harry Bransons, newlyweds from Indiana, had built a pool hall, barbershop, haberdashery combination business on a lot northwest of our house. They also built a house across the alley from us on the next street west. They were relatives of the Speeces. There were a lot of settlers from Indiana in our town. Harry soon brought his brother Carey to help, as he had more business than he could handle alone.

In the fall, a freight car was shunted onto the railroad siding, and people came from all over the countryside to buy barrels of apples. Father always bought two barrels to store in our pantry, and it was wonderful to have an apple, evenings during the winter. Later, another freight car came in loaded with sacks of frozen flounder. We got several sacks and kept them frozen in the pumphouse, to be eaten during the winter.

Neighbors began asking Charlie if they could connect to our water system. At first, there were only a few, and the system handled them nicely. But more neighbors kept asking, and Father never could say "No" to any of them. One family even hooked in without asking. Finally we had ten customers, and it was far too great a load for the water system to carry. We began to receive frequent calls for water on the telephone. Charlie was away all day on his road foreman's job, so Axel, Donald, and I had to take the responsibility of keeping our customers supplied with water, by running the pump engine and checking the water pressure.

But occasionally we would slip away for a swim or a fishing expedition to the Whiteface River. Ground hog burrows began to appear in our hay field, and they spread rapidly. It worried Father as the ground hogs were eating a ot of clover. He bought us a single shot .22 caliber rifle. It was an accurate little gun, with a fine sight and a longer than average barrel. He told us that he would pay twentyfive cents for every groundhog tail we brought to him from an animal shot on our land. We started off haphazardly trying to shoot them, but we found that if one was shot anywhere but in the brain, it would flop into its hole and crawl back out of reach, so we could never secure its tail. By watching the groundhog's habits, I devised a plan for hunting them. They are by nature a curious animal. When approached, they will quickly crawl down into their burrow. But in a short time they have just got to find out what is going on above ground. I would approach a burrow and watch the quarry dive into its hole. Then I'd lie down within range and wait, my rifle trained on the entrance. Before long the groundhog's head would reappear, just high enough to survey the vicinity. That was all I needed and my success rate soared. I began to save the tails, and one day I brought twelve of them to Father for payment. He paid me in accordance with our agreement, but he said, "That's enough for now." We continued to hunt them for sport now and then. For the time being they were pretty well cleaned out of our meadow.

The new President, Warren Harding, promised us a return to "Normalcy," but for farmers, the Depression began in nineteen twenty-two. They had enough to eat, of course, home grown, but the prices for oats dropped to thirty cents a bushel; wheat went to forty-five cents, and the price of cream was very low. Potatoes went from thirty cents a bushel up to a dollar one year. That year, Peter Roth had a bumper crop. He had so many potatoes that he dumped them in enormous piles in the middle of his field hoping for a rise in price to one dollar and twenty-five cents. The weather turned frosty, and he covered them with straw. Suddenly a sub-zero blast of wind swept in from the north and froze the piles of potatoes solid. The next year potatoes sold for thirty cents again, and there was scarcely any market for them. Year after year, Lillian, Axel, Donald, and I would cut enough seed potatoes for a few acres, hoe them, hill, and harvest them. We'd store them in our cellar, covered with tar paper and straw, using a few bushels for our table. In the spring we'd start the same process over again, throwing the surplus out in the fields to rot.

Meanwhile, sister Margie was beginning to toddle about, and she became the center of our affections. In the afternoon, she loved to be rocked to sleep. When Mother was too busy, she sometimes delegated me to do the job. It started out smoothly enough, but gradually developed into a hilarious game. I would rock as hard as I could, meanwhile swing my head about and shouting "Na, Na, Na," imitating Mother but in a ridiculous fashion. Margie and I would end up laughing, and all chances of her napping would be forgotten.

Our Mother, Lydia, Mrs. Schleinitz, Mrs. John Murker, and Mrs. Ervin Sausman were great pals. They loved to get together over coffee and rolls, and talk. Careful record was kept of their birthdays, which always meant coffee and cake at the honored one's home. They laughingly called themselves the "Big Four," and there was some truth in the title since they each weighed somewhere between one hundred seventy and one hundred ninety pounds.

CHAPTER IV

Parties

The "Big Four" were gathered at our house one year for Mother's birthday and were sitting in our living room enjoying themselves when there was a knock at the back door. Mother went through the kitchen and opened it. A group of Finnish ladies had decided to come and give her a surprise birthday party. She invited them in and found chairs in the kitchen for them. Her attempts to speak to them in English met with no success. It seemed they only talked Finnish. Mother was in a quandary. Should she take them in to the living room and introduce them to the "Big Four" How would they communicate? For the Finnish ladies this was also to be a get acquainted party as well, so Lydia didn't know all of their names.

In a short time the Finnish ladies began to realize that a party was already in progress, so they wished Mother a happy birthday and departed. They never came back again. She had lost a chance to renew ties with people from Finland and must have regretted the way it turned out.

One evening the "Big Four" were invited to go on a hayride party out to the home of the Christ Nelsons, one mile north of town. They had decided to dress in their husbands' coveralls or overalls for the trip. The hayrack and horse were provided by Mrs. Nelson, who drove into town to pick them up. To make the journey longer and presumably more exciting, they decided to drive west, one half mile, then north one mile to the Landgren's corner and finally eastward one half mile to the Nelson home. They had hardly gotten underway when the husbands started plotting. They got into a Model T Ford, drove to the Nelsons', and went into action. After hiding the Ford behind the barn ! they caught two pigs and barricaded them in the parlor under the table. Then they filled the house with chickens and fastened tin cans to the outside window sills. Twine was run from holes in the bottoms of the cans to some nearby bushes, and the twine was covered with rosin. Then they hid in the bushes to wait.

It was nearly dark when the ladies arrived. The men said that when the women entered the house, it sounded "like all hell had broken loose!" The pigs had gotten out from under the table. There was a mixture of screaming, squealing, and squawking as pigs and chickens were driven out the back door.

By that time it was dark. The men started rubbing the rosined twine. Weird honking noises came from the tin cans attached to the windows. Screaming and laughing, the women emerged to peer into the darkness. Hidden in the bushes lay the culprits, quiet while the search went on. Later, it was said, the men walked in by way of the road and denied having anything to do with what happened.

Big changes were occurring in Meadowlands. The new creamery was in operation. Harry Branson brought in an electric light plant from Dakota, and he started a telephone system. Everyone in town had electric lights. Father bought one of those new electrically driven, wringer-type washing machines called a Waterwitch from Montgomery Ward. It would last for twenty-four years, with only a change of wringer rolls when they wore out. It surely lightened Mother's washing labors. Beside numerous dwellings, a Catholic church was constructed. Subscribers got together and put up a community hall for social activities. Passenger trains went through twice a day both to Duluth and to the Iron Range towns. Iron ore trains, a mile long, pulled by enormous Malley engines, roared through day and night taking ore to the loading docks in Duluth. Several times a year, the grownups would entrain for Duluth to see a play at the Orpheum Theater. A favorite pastime for the young men and women was to "meet the train," that is, to go to the depot to see who came into town or who was going away.

A new type of phonograph was becoming popular. It played flat disk records, and the horn or speaker was enclosed within the box. People were continually buying the latest hits. The Speeces had a player piano that played music automatically when you put a roll in the mountings and pumped two pedals with your feet. One evening in 1922, Gilbert "Bud" Lowe, the depot agent's son, invited Axel and me over for a game of cards. It was a comical game, and we laughed and enjoyed ourselves. But at eight o'clock, Bud put the cards away and brought out a wooden box with a set headphones attached. He plugged wires into an outlet leading to an aerial that was out on the roof. Putting on the head piece, he began to turn some dials on the box. Then he took the headset from his head, detached the earphones, and handed one to Axel and one to me. Listening, we learned that the music was coming from Buffalo, New York, being played by Vincent Lopez and his orchestra. Unbelievable, but there it was. The radio was a two-tube set, and it had cost two hundred dollars. It was the first radio in our town. Years would pass before we owned one. By that time speakers were installed inside, more tubes were added, and the sets were much cheaper to buy.

In the spring of nineteen hundred twenty-three, the girls in our school grades decided to have a party. For some time they had shown more interest in the boys, smiling and engaging us in conversation. We were eleven or twelve years of age by that time and were somewhat embarrassed by all of this attention. The boys were confused but flattered by their attentions. We still preferred the company of our male companions. The evening of the party, we boys walked out to the Christ Nelson home expecting to play the usual games such as "drop the handkerchief," with a lunch to follow. When we arrived and entered, we were surprised to find that all of the furniture and carpets had been removed from the living room except for the piano and a piano stool.

With all guests present, Mrs. Nelson sat down at the piano and began to play dance music. One by one the boys got "chosen" by a girl. Dancing instructions began: one step, two steps, and waltzes. It was an awkward, jerky process at first, but finally we mastered some of the dance steps, and a certain rhythm and smoothness began evolve. One piece Mrs. Nelson played, "The Love Ship," we especially liked. We boys began to take a certain pride in our dancing ability. We began to ask the girls to dance. It was late when we started to walk home, boys with boys and girls with girls, of course! We would never be caught walking home with a girl.

Somehow we would never be quite the same again. Perhaps the girls had, by stealth and trickery, forced us to begin growing up. Girls mature ahead of boys. It is possible we were coming on so slowly that they decided what we needed was a shove. A new dimension had been added to our lives. The boys had to acknowledge that such a thing as a boy-girl relationship did indeed exist.

CHAPTER V

Progress

With World War I ended, the citizenry turned their interest once again toward occupations of a country at peace. Farmers cleared more land and sold the logs for lumber or paper pulp. They built new homes and barns to replace the makeshift buildings erected for temporary shelter in the early years. Large areas of land were ditched with dredges to lower the water level, so it could be farmed. To the northwest of town, on a half section of cleared land, an experimental and demonstration farm was soon in operation, complete with farmhouse, two large barns, bunkhouses for the help, and even a dinner bell to bring them in from the fields at mealtime. It was a beautiful layout, but it must have been expensive.

The Meadowlands area ringed by forests and situated on land between the confluence of the Whiteface and St. Louis rivers, provided fishing, hunting, trapping, skating, and skiing as recreation for us, the first generation to grow up in its confines. For these activities we had no teachers. We learned to swim or to handle guns on a trial and error basis. If our parents worried about us, they didn't show it or say anything except, "Be careful!" We developed a sense of caution ourselves as a result and took no chances in our primeval playground. A few who didn't paid the price for their carelessness.

The railway companies had received grants of nearly one million acres of land adjacent to track systems constructed from Duluth to the Iron Range, every other section of land, as partial compensation for building costs incurred. However, much of the best acreage in the area had already been homesteaded or sold to early settlers. Forest fires during nineteen nineteen had leveled new tracts of land, and it looked like very little effort would be required to prepare them for cultivation. Unimproved land was selling for thirty-five or forty dollars per acre. Railroad authorities estimated that improved land, cleared, and plowed, ready for crops could bring in about one hundred and twenty-five dollars an acre. It looked like a profitable venture, so a land improvement and sales organization was established. Pilot programs were unknown at the time. Such a program on a limited scale could have proved or disproved the validity of the organization's estimates. Lacking such information, the land development agency inaugurated a full scale land development program. It soon ran into serious difficulties. Beneath the burned-over areas were millions of tree roots and stumps, and the land was wet and soft. Large portions of acreage were composed of peat bog, unsuitable for crop production. Undaunted, the land department imported gigantic Caterpillar tractors and immense plows to tear out the stumps and turn the soil. The big tractors often bogged down, and the plows broke. A large repair shop was built near the depot in Meadowlands to handle equipment repair. The project plunged forward, and several hundred acres of land were opened up for production but at a tremendous cost. Some of it proved sour, and it required lime. The higher peat lands under cultivation were not very fertile and required a full complement of fertilizers.

Two large buildings were constructed along the railway tracks, one for potato storage and the other for packing lettuce and cauliflower. In addition to inducing farmers to plant lettuce, the land department went into lettuce production itself. Large quantities of lettuce were iced and packed in crates for shipment to Chicago. For a time it seemed that the whole land project was well launched, that it would continue to grow. Its effect on Meadowlands was good. There were plenty of jobs for the young men. The boys of our age were paid fifteen cents an hour to help ready lettuce for packing, evenings after our farm work was finished. Everyone was optimistic. Community activities were humming;

dances were held regularly in the town hall, and we built a tennis court over cinders provided by the railroad company. The big lettuce packing building was dedicated by holding a dance with an orchestra from Duluth. The railroad president arrived in a special railroad car to attend the dance and remain overnight.

Meanwhile, prices for cream, butter, cheese, eggs, potatoes, and grain remained almost at cost level. Some farmers took their produce to the Hibbing farmer's market twice a week and sold it directly to consumers for a fair profit. They also raised a great variety of stuff for their own consumption, both animal and vegetable. Those who diversified fared the best.

The sport of baseball was revived, along with the Fourth of July celebrations and a town fair. A new innovation was sweeping the country. It was an organization called the Boy Scouts. Almost overnight we were organized into a troop, complete with suits in the pattern of World War I soldier's uniforms. Someone must have put pressure on Father to buy uniforms for Axel and me because we got them without even having to ask.

It was Memorial Day, 1923, and the town was saturated with patriotism. We had only recently fought the war which ended all wars. To commemorate our war dead, a march was organized. We began by hoisting a flag in the park. Then, lead by our Spanish American war veteran on his spirited horse, his sword swinging at his side, the inhabitants commenced a march, first southward, then eastward one mile to the cemetery. Our scout troop was situated somewhere in the mass of marchers. There must have been two hundred people in all!

As we neared the railroad tracks, the passenger train passed in front of us on its way to the depot. It gave us a couple of extra toots as it roared past. I remember wondering what the passengers must think of us, a stream of humanity solemnly following an old man on horseback out into the country. We stopped for a few minutes at the Whiteface River bridge, while a paper boat filled with flowers was lowered by strings into the water. We expected it to float with all dignity downstream, but it sank, all but the bow and the flowers, so we went to the graveyard to decorate the graves of friends and relatives. Our town had no casualties from World War I. In fact only five men got overseas before the war ended.

In nineteen twenty-three! E. Z. Marks brought several carloads of horses to town on the railroad, and his cowboys unloaded them into the corral. They were wild horses off of the plains of Montana. Farmers came from far and wide to bid and sales were brisk. The cowboys knew their trade. They would lay their loop on the ground, drive the desired animal past. and zip the loop flashed out. The horse would run his head right through the loop. Father bought Dolly, a small black horse for riding and cultivating. She didn't like to be caught, so I learned the cowboy's flip, and it worked most of the time.

The Speeces were from Indiana, and most of them lived one mile north of town on two farms called Speeceville. Indiana is corn, hog, and watermelon country. Everyone in Meadowlands knew that it was too far north to raise watermelons. The growing season was too short. But the Speeces wouldn't give up. Year after year, they would plant watermelon seeds, but before the melons ripened, a heavy frost would turn the leaves black. However in nineteen twenty-three there was an early spring, a hot summer, and a late fall. There were many large piles of ripe watermelon behind Speece's barn. Nate Sanders was also from Indiana, and his son Rex was my classmate. He knew all about watermelon.

They were holding a town meeting in the hall, and farmers came in from all over to attend, including the Speeces. I was loafing along Main Street about seven o'clock in the evening pondering what to do. To me the meeting would be a boring affair. Suddenly, Sander's Model T, "June Bug," drew up alongside. Rex was driving and he was alone.

He said, "Hey, Vic!" I looked up and said, "Hi, Rex." He motioned me over to the car.

"Do you like watermelon?"

"I sure do."

"C'mon. Get in."

I got in. Rex drove the auto west, then northward past the

railroad tracks. He drifted to the side of the road, stopped, and switched off the lights.

"C'mon," he said again. I got out and followed him. We cut east, across Speece's field. It was so dark we could hardly see. Suddenly, we were among those piles of watermelon. Rex went around thumping them with his finger. "Take this one," he said handing it to me. He thumped a few more and selected one for himself. We headed back for the "Bug." Speece's dog slept on. We drove back a little ways toward town, stopped again, and cut wedges from the first melon. We cut wedges and ate until finally we couldn't stand the sight of watermelon anymore. Rex let me out in town and took off for home. It was some time before I could eat watermelon again and like it.

Swiping strawberries or corn or chickens was considered a lark. We lived in town, but our strawberries and corn were planted on the farm one-fourth of a mile south. Sometimes after dark, people would come rushing up to one of us and say "There are some flashlights going up and down the rows of strawberries (or corn) on your farm." Of course, they wanted us to take a shotgun, go out there, and fire a few blasts in the air, while boys and girls would go screaming, to hide or get away. It would have been fun, but we never did do it.

That fall, the threshers pulled into our farmyard. Father backed the old Waterloo Boy tractor around in line with the thresher pulley, slipped the belt on, and we started threshing oats. I alternated between straw pusher and waterboy that morning. The band cutter had to leave for the afternoon, so I took over the job of cutting twine on the bundles, before Dan Johnson, the feeder, threw them into the machine. Dan was a tall Swede with hands like hams. Before we started work, he looked down at me and told me this story.

"Y'know, when I was out in Dakota threshing grain once, the boy who was cutting bands cut the feeder's hand. The feeder grabbed the boy and threw him into the thresher." I was only thirteen and had to reach up on the table to cut the bands. Believe me, I was mighty careful not to cut Dan's hands! But I was outraged by the treatment received by the poor band cutter that had cut the feeder's hands. Finally, after we had completed the threshing, I asked Dan, "What did they do to that man who threw the boy into the threshing machine?" He looked at me and said, "Well, they unhooked a team of horses from a wagon, leaving the singletrees attached to the harness and faced one horse east and the other west. They tied one of the man's legs to one singletree and the other leg to the singletree; then they said, 'Giddap!'"

The next day we pulled into Lewis Miller's, and the threshing went on. It looked like we'd finish by 2 o'clock in the afternoon, so we worked right on through noon hour. At two o'clock, with the job done, we unhooked, and went to their house for dinner. The house had a long, open porch across the back. We dipped water out of a barrel into a basin, soaped up from a bar of soap, and washed our hands and faces, drying with a towel on a nail nearby.

There was a long table, and three women were busy with the dinner preparations. When we were all seated, they brought in great bowls of fried chicken, potatoes, pickles, and vegetables. There was bread, milk, coffee, and to top off the meal, large slabs of pie. I never will forget that meal or how much we ate. It was delicious and practically all from home grown ingredients!

That fall Lillian had to go to Hibbing to finish high school as there was no fourth year established in the Meadowlands High School. She worked for the Murphys during that year, then went to Duluth for her year at Normal school, preparing to become a teacher.

Grandma Sarah died in the summer of nineteen twenty-two. In the language of the times, it probably would have been said she died of old age. As Grandpa Fredrick was buried in Turtle Lake, all of the elders made the trek there with her body to place it beside her husband. Photographs were taken of the family as it was the custom. They reveal a somber group, the survivors.

Then Werner married Edda Speece. They moved across the street. Werner worked full time at his garage, and Father was kept busy on the county roads. Axel and I kept on with the farming, with

Donald growing up to help us. Then Father put Axel to work running the tractor that pulled the road grading machine while he operated the grader. The reason he put Axel on the county tractor job was that no one else wanted it. The standard wage in Meadowlands was one dollar per hour, but the county only paid fifty cents per hour for the tractor operator. So for much of the time, the farm work fell on the shoulders of Donald and me. Father and Axel helped whenever possible. For really big jobs Father would hire help.

The Olson and Peterson saw mill opened that year. It was the beginning of a local logging and lumber industry, requiring more help. The temptation was great among students in the first year of high school to quit school to earn one dollar an hour. A few did quit to become loggers, but most continued their education. Aunt Anna quit her job at the local bank to marry Frank Zanker. They seemed so happy. Then suddenly she was dead. It was a toxic condition involving her pregnancy. It was said nothing could be done for her, but her son was saved. Named Warren, he was given to his father's sister to raise. Anna too, was buried at Turtle Lake.

Mr. Bond, the school superintendent, was Latin I teacher during my first year of high school. He was short, rather heavy, with pince nez glasses and black, curly hair parted in the middle. He was intelligent, well bred, and an excellent teacher. For some reason, all of the school board members were women. It is doubtful if any of them had more than an eighth grade education, but they sought to instill a bit of culture in us by marching us to the church to hear a quartet of their group sing. They stood stiffly in a row by the piano, their eyes fixed on a spot in the northwest corner of the ceiling and rendered, among other selections, "The Battle Hymn of the Republic." — Then we were marched back to the school.

For reasons known only to themselves, our woman school board refused to rehire Mr. Bond for the coming year. He was well liked by the community at large and by the students. When news of the board's action travelled through the area, people were outraged. But it was too late to help save Mr. Bond for our school. That fall, the women on the school board were voted out by an overwhelming majority. When the ballots were counted and the results given out, there was a parade of automobiles, blowing their horns and circling in the streets. For a long time afterwards, only men became members of the school board.

Mrs. Max Schleinitz stood looking out of the front window of the store recently purchased from H. C. Hansen. She saw Mr. and Mrs. Sneller from Stony Point drive up, stop their horse, and Mr. Sneller came into the store. Mrs. Sneller got out of the wagon also, but instead of following Mr. Sneller, she got a bag from the wagon and walked to the ditch across the street. She began to pick up pieces of scrap tin foil and colored paper, putting them into the bag. Mrs. Schleinitz stood watching, mystified by this performance. Finally, curiosity overcame her, and she went out of the store and crossed to where Mrs. Sneller was busy gathering choice bits of trash and stuffing them into her bag.

"Why are you picking up that stuff, Mrs. Sneller?" she asked. "Because I'm crazy," replied Mrs. Sneller. After a moment's pause, Mrs. Schleinitz asked, "Are you going to sell it?" "Oh! I'm not that crazy," replied Mrs. Sneller. It is possible that Mrs. Schleinitz felt one couldn't argue with logic like that. She turned and went back into the store.

Now that prohibition laws were in effect, whiskey, wine, and beer could not be purchased legally. It did not, however, prohibit making one's own liquor for home consumption. The German community in Elmer gained a reputation for making the best grape wine. They bought grapes by the dozens of crates, making enough wine in casks to last all year. The Swedes excelled at makinq beer. We tried a batch or two with only mediocre results, so we gave it up. One summer we decided to make five gallons of dandelion wine. We followed the recipe exactly, setting the batch in a five gallon crock. When it was ready, we put it in a large jug to age for two months. But brother Axel couldn't seem to leave it alone. He started to pour out a little to taste, now and then. Before long he was draining a quart at a time to take for his buddies to "taste."

When the two months aging time was past, we went down to draw a bottle of wine. We found that there were only settlings left in the bottom of the jug. We decided to get even with Axel and let Werner and everyone else in on our scheme. We mixed about a pound of Epson Salts in a gallon of water, poured this mixture into the wine jug, and mixed it well with the settlings.

The gang was sitting on Werner's and Edna's porch when Werner said to Axel, "Say, Axel, we've heard about that good dandelion wine that you all made, but we haven't even tasted a drop of it." Axel answered, "Oh? Well, I'll go right over and pour out a bottle of it and bring it over. It'll only take a minute."

Axel was back shortly, the glasses were all ready, so he proceeded to fill a glass for everyone, including himself, of course. Everyone pretended to sip their wine, saying how good it was. Axel sipped his wine too but seemed quite puzzled. As they moved around the porch, when Axel was looking the other way, one, then another would dash their drink out through the screen. Finally their glasses were all empty, Axel still had a little left in his. He tossed it off, saying, "Ya know, that tastes just like Epsom Salts." It was all they could do to maintain sober faces. When they told him what they had done the next day, he was angry, but no more was said about the wine. We never tried to make it again.

Dan Phillips was brought in from California to instruct the local people in making lettuce crates and packing them for shipment. He was a young, handsome bachelor admired by the young ladies, but after the season was over, he returned to California.

Paul Sramek became land agent for the land department. He moved to Meadowlands with his wife and child and started a campaign selling land to his own compatriots, the Czechoslovak people. Soon there was a regular colony of Czechs living in the area. They formed a Sokol Society, built a hall in the country, and gave dances, gymnastic events, and celebrations in native Czech costumes. Being of agricultural background, this group rooted well and succeeded in their farming projects.

At intervals, Mother received letters from Finland. They contained news of deaths in the family; first, her father , then her mother, and finally her sister, Rosa. After reading the letters, she would shed tears for a moment, wipe her eyes, and get on with her work. There was so much to be done, and one could grieve while working. She seldom heard from her sisters anymore.

Sandra wrote about her life on the farm at Gheen. One winter night, when her husband August was away in his logging camp, the toothache which plagued her became unbearable. After doing the barn chores, she set out on a country road and walked many miles to a railway flag station in the dark. She flagged the train and boarded it to Virginia. After the tooth was extracted, she caught the return train, got off at the flag station, and walked back home.

One summer day, Sandra had a problem. The men were busy out in the fields putting up the hay crop, and there was no meat to prepare for their dinner. She went out to the barn, selected a calf, led it to a convenient spot and butchered it. The haymakers had their meal on time!

It was nineteen twenty-five, and Father bought a half ton Model T Ford truck. Father couldn't drive a car at first, so we boys learned, again by trial and error. Luckily we made no errors. Lillian finished her one year normal school teaching course and got a teaching position at a small one room school west of Cook, Minnesota, about seventy-five miles away from Meadowlands. Axel and I were assigned to drive her to the school. We located it without any problems and then found the widow's farm, one mile distant from the school, where Lillian was to live. The widow, an ancient little lady was also to prepare her meals, and Lillian would walk to and from school each day. It soon turned out that the only fruit she got at mealtime was wild raspberries that had been picked from bushes nearby. Occasionally, Lillian was served wild partridge, and she wondered where they came from since the widow never went hunting them. Then one day she saw the widow's cat dragging a partridge home from the woods. Sure enough, the next day they had partridge for dinner. That ended Lillian's stay with the widow. She moved in with the Carlsons in Cook, and thereafter, was driven to school by one of the Carlson boys. Mrs. Carlson, by the way, was the same person who had operated the Svea Hotel in Virginia. Lillian enjoyed her stay with the Carlsons, but she was transferred to Palo, Minnesota, the following year.

CHAPTER VI

Conservation

About seven miles south of Meadowlands stood a magnificent stand of virgin pine trees that had somehow escaped the nineteen nineteen forest fires. The stand was estimated at six million board feet of timber. In the fall of nineteen twenty-five, large camp buildings were constructed of pine logs to house a hundred or more lumberjacks and about forty horses. A large cook shack was built for preparing and serving meals. It was called "Cloudy's Camp" after the camp boss, J. P. Cloudy. I caught a ride to see the camp one day when Father and a truck driver graded the roads in that direction. We stopped at the cook shack and were invited in for a large bowl of coffee and big pieces of pie. We were impressed by the size of the camp and the enormous horses standing in the barn. With the arrival of cold weather and snow, ice roads were prepared to haul logs to the St. Louis River two or three miles away. The logs were loaded upon large bob sleds and were hauled to the river where they were unloaded onto the river ice. Eventually the ice broke and logs filled the river bed clear to the bottom for a quarter mile's distance. The unloading continued until the whole river valley was filled.

Every pine tree was cut and hauled away, leaving not one to provide seed for new growth. Slashings were left on the ground where they fell.

When the trees were all harvested and hauled to the river, logs used to build the camp were also cut and moved to the pile on the St. Louis. By springtime of nineteen twenty-six there was only a cleared space among the spruce trees where the camp had stood.

One Sunday afternoon I went with some friends in a Model T truck to see the camp, but it was gone. We got on the ice road and drove to the St. Louis River to see the harvested logs. They were something to see. We wondered how the loggers could get them started down the river to the mills in Cloquet. But later, the melting snow took care of that. Dammed by the log mass the river rose high in the riverbed. The logs began to move urged on by lumberjacks with pike poles and cant hooks. It was the last big log drive in the Midwest. The big pine forest was gone. Fifty years later, I toured the area to see if any pine survived the logging operation. The area is still a wilderness covered with spruce, maple, and aspen. But I didn't see one pine tree. In recent years, large lumbering interests are spending huge sums of money advertising their conservation programs. I could not possibly believe their claims until I see a stand of pine again growing where it once grew seven miles south of Meadowlands.

The community continued to grow. There were plenty of jobs for those who wanted to work. Farmers that found it hard to keep up payments on their lands took jobs on the side, while helping their wives and children with the farm work on weekends.

Leaders in the community decided that it was time to incorporate the townsite area into a village, and this was completed in nineteen twenty-five. Father was elected to be the first mayor. To an outsider he probably would have seemed a unusual choice.

Standing about five feet, seven inches in height, slightly rounded shoulders, quite heavy, with a paunchy waist, he could be seen around the village in his off hours, chatting anyone who came along, stopping on occasion to open his snuffbox and place a chew in his mouth. He was natural, easily approachable, and ready to listen to anyone's troubles, offering sympathy, advice, or just friendly conversation. In the summer he wore pants and a blue shirt or else a suit of coveralls. In winter he changed to heavy black trousers, heavy shirt, and jacket, with mittens, and a Scotch cap, and heavy, lumberjack lined boots. The mayor's post offered no salary, and he seemed to attach no importance to it.

Some of the inhabitants had purchased new automobiles.

One Sunday a pair of identical Kissel cars drove out into center and parked at the baseball diamond before the ball game commenced, but they were from some other community and were not seen again. With the approach of Fair Day, posters appeared in store windows announcing that an airplane was coming to town to sell rides. A field west of town was provided for the event. The field was also to be dedicated as an emergency landing place for aircraft in times of distress. Father was asked to be there for the dedication in his capacity as mayor of Meadowlands. He went out to the field, and at about nine-thirty in the morning, a two-seater airplane landed, piloted by "Dusty" Rhoades. He taxied up to where a group of people awaited. An official looking document was handed to Father which proclaimed that the farm was an emergency landing field. "Dusty" then had Charlie don a flier's jacket and helmet so that pictures could be taken to commemorate the occasion. The pictures duly taken, "Dusty" announced to one and all that to show that flying was safe and to show appreciation for the generous dedication of the field, he was going to take the mayor on the first ride, free. It is probable that the last thing that Father wanted was an airplane ride, free or otherwise. But there he stood with every one looking on. How could he refuse? He was soon aboard and strapped in. The airplane scudded around on its tail iron and taxied up the field. Then with a mighty roar, it raced down the bumpy turf and finally was airborne. When it landed, Father climbed down, a bit frozen of face and wobbly of knee, glad to feel the solid earth under his feet again. Many rides, at three dollars for five minutes, were sold that day. The barnstorming operation was declared a success. When father arrived home, he gave Axel and me three dollars apiece. But he advised us that it would be better if we didn't ride on the airplane. We obeyed.

By nineteen twenty-five almost everyone owned a phonograph. The newest recorded hits were continually being purchased, and as improvements were made on radios, they too, began to appear in homes. Broadcasting was gradually becoming a big business. A new style of music called jazz was sweeping the country, and it changed the mode of dancing. Waltzes became less popular. Polkas, Schotteiches, and square dances became extinct, except among older people. During the twenties, more music was composed of pieces which later were called "standards" for their beauty and durability than any time before or since, in America. Compositions of good merit flowed easily from composer to recorder to the public. The time had not yet arrived when music would be dominated by big business, to be stifled by song pluggers offering inferior selections.

The land department sent four young men to the Agricultural School at the University of Minnesota in St. Paul for a three months crash course on farming techniques. What they learned at the school was problematical. But one thing they learned during the off hours was how to do the "Charleston." After graduation they returned to Meadowlands decked out in bell- bottomed trousers and immediately began to instruct the natives in the new dance. It was the rage for about two weeks, but being a novelty dance, it was soon forgotten. The older folk listened to the new jazz improvisations with some suspicion. It was rumored that a saxophone player could be fined or jailed for jazzing "Dardanella" on his instrument. Meanwhile the farmers continued to eke out a bare living on their farms. Prices for their produce remained low. Ray Greiten took over as farm supervisor for the land department. He continued with the lettuce production program, sending carloads of lettuce to Chicago, where it stood sidetracked until it spoiled, and a bill was received for railroad car demurrage. The lettuce raising project came to a halt. Axel decided to "join the Navy and see the world" as the slogans read. Six years later, he came out of the navy a full-fledged machinist, a trade that was to be a great help to him in later life. Donald, Father, and I took over whatever occasional duties he performed on the farm. Father had built a new barn and was starting a herd of Guernsey milk cows .

Uncle Andrew had been in and out of the Veterans Administration hospital in Minneapolis since World War I. His lungs, damaged by the mustard gas, bothered him constantly. He was also bored by months lying in hospital beds. Periodically, he would sneak away, to be gone for several months only to return in bad condition. His final escape in nineteen twenty-six brought him to a hotel in Duluth where he gradually weakened and died. Once more, there was a gathering of the family in Turtle Lake where he was laid to rest beside his mother and father. There was a government life insurance policy left behind. Father was Andrew's estate administrator. He divided the money equally between the remaining brothers but included one equal share for Anna's child, Warren.

Father wanted to pay his share of the insurance money for the farm mortgage, but Werner, his brother did not want to do so with his share. It was therefore decided that the farming partnership be dissolved. Father took over the northwest forty, secured his deed, and retired the mortgage. Werner continued ownership of the east forty but left it mortgaged. For some reason, Father and Werner had borrowed five hundred dollars from Uncle Fred, giving him title to the south forty acres. But Father continued to pay taxes on this forty and to use it for pasture. Since the original one hundred and twenty acres were purchased for six thousand, five hundred dollars, it is difficult to understand why Uncle Fred was given title to the south forty for only five hundred dollars. Perhaps Father was cast in the role of father figure again, taking care of his "Family." What ever the reason, it will never be known. Fred was away operating locomotives again, and we continued to pay his taxes and pasture his forty.

The railroad land improvement and sales venture began to falter. With low farm prices and in some commodities, no market at all, some farmers were defaulting on their land payments. Many had started with little or no money, signed a purchase agreement, and hoped to make their payments out of crops harvested. Railroad supervisors began to take a closer look at the whole land project. Clearing and plowing land for sale was discontinued. Little by little, activities were curtailed until only the salesman, Mr. Sramek, was retained to sell land in its natural state. As a result of the change in the land sales policy, many young men lost their jobs. There was a gradual exodus of these workers to the city or to other states. A few settlers continued to buy land, based upon

97

lower selling prices, and set about clearing their own croplands. But the forward and upward impetus of the area had peaked out.

In nineteen twenty-five, the school board had added a fourth high school year, so a class of five seniors graduated in June of nineteen twenty-six, when I was a junior. There was talk about some of them going on to college. The subject was revived the following year among our senior class of four students. It seemed to be the only goal for us, with jobs almost nonexistent for graduates in Meadowlands. But Father didn't see the need for anyone spending four years in college. The time and money would be wasted. When the subject was broached, he kept silent. I gave up all hope of continuing my education.

High school graduation exercises were held for our class in the town hall. We graduates were seated in the front of the stage, facing the speaker hired to give the commencement address. The hall behind us was filled to the last row with relatives and friends.

After a few preliminaries, the speaker, a small man with white hair, rose and began his address. He said, "You know that we are all millionaires, all of us, you, you, and you. We're all millionaires." He paused to let the statement sink in. "We're millionaires in brain cells." He went on for a moment extolling brain cells. Then he said, "You see our hair not only grows outward. It grows inward too, and when the roots strike grey matter, the hair turns grey. However, if it doesn't find any gray matter, it falls out."

The audience roared, and looked around to grin at the red-faced baldies seated in the hall. When the speaker finished, we were awarded our certificates, and the exercise was brought to a close. For me, that summer, it meant the termination of schooling. Not once was further education for me discussed.

BOOK III

CHAPTER I

Studies and Jazz

Two days before enrollment at Hibbing Junior College, I returned from the farm, walked into the kitchen, and hung my cap on the rack behind the door. Mother said, " You'd better start getting your things ready. You're going to college." I couldn't believe it! No talk, no plans, and suddenly it was a reality. How did it happen? Had Mother and Lillian persuaded Father to let me go? He could not, surely, have made the decision by himself. I was sure that he had yielded under persuasion, but I said nothing, fearing that even mentioning the subject might reverse the decision.

There was the matter of clothing. I had one suit, a fair pair of shoes, and a hat, besides some well-used shirts, socks, and underwear. From Uncle Andrew, I had inherited unofficially, an overcoat. He had been a tailor, and it was a good coat, albeit, a bit out of fashion.

Axel, Lillian, and I drove to Hibbing in the Model T truck on the day before registration began. We stopped at a men's clothing store where I purchased a heavy pullover sweater. It was to be my second skin for two years. Then we drove to the home where I was to stay during my first year of junior college. It was owned by a family who had formerly lived near my parents' home in Pool Location before we moved to Meadowlands. There we unloaded my bag, and I entered, to be greeted by the owner's wife. She showed me to the room that I was to share with her oldest son. My clothes stowed away, we returned downstairs.

Lillian and Axel said good-bye and were soon going around the corner in the Model T Ford. I stood at the screen door, pressing my nose and forehead against the screen to watch them out of sight.

I was to have only my breakfast with the family during each day that year, but on this first evening, I was asked to have dinner with them. Soon, my roommate, a senior in high school and his brother arrived and we sat to eat. They eyed me curiously, and I wondered what they were looking at me so strangely. Suddenly the mother asked, "What have you got on your face? Your forehead and nose are black." Then I remembered putting my face against the screen. We laughed while I cleaned the dust from my face. My roommate turned out to be a fine fellow, easy to get along with, and full of fun. He worked evenings at a butcher shop, so I was free to use the one writing desk in our room whenever writing was required. The junior college was located only three blocks' distance away, in the west wing of the massive building that housed South Hibbing High School. There were only about two hundred students enrolled in the college. They came from Duluth, Proctor, Two Harbors, Nashwawk, Chisholm, and Buhl as well as Hibbing itself, with only one or two of us from farming areas.

The first day at school was devoted to registration, assignment to counselors, course selection, and distribution of books and study materials. One by one, we sat with our counselor, and our curriculum for the semester was prescribed. My counselor was Mr. Drescher, a chemistry teacher. He scanned my high school credits and noticed no chemistry and no foreign language. "That must be remedied," he said. I was placed in a six hour per week chemistry course along with students who had already studied chemistry while in high school, some of which were going into medicine or dentistry. He also placed me in a French class along with a group of students who had completed high school French. I didn't know what I was getting into, in those classes. There were two other classes, English and economics, where I had some previous high school background.

High schools of the Range towns were superb. Supported by a tax base founded on rich iron ore deposits of the area, they offered a great variety of regular and unique courses, as well as sports and music. They hired the best teachers, paid the highest salaries, and provided the grandest auditoriums in the state. Coming from the little high school in Meadowlands, I had not even begun to realize how ill prepared I was. I learned about it as the year progressed.

What is to be said about college studies? Not much. Because of my sparse background in chemistry and French, I had to work very hard in these subjects for mediocre grades. But English, where I was better prepared, came easily, and I garnered an "A" in that subject. Grades in psychology were a toss-up. The students said that our psychology teacher threw our tests up the stairs. Those that slid down the farthest got low grades, and those that stuck farther up, got higher grades. But he was a high grader, so we didn't worry about our grades in that course.

Occasionally my roommate and I walked over to Brooklyn addition where dances were held upstairs in the fire hall. There was usually a five or six piece orchestra: accordion, drums, trumpet, saxophone, and clarinet. They were always good. The latest jazz selections were played in a scorching rhythm geared to our bouncing eighteen year old tastes. Much has been made of jazz originating in the south. But it never really acquired finesse and interpretive innovation until it spread up north and to California. The Charleston had already died a sudden death. It was never danced by more than a few people, and most didn't like it, despite later claims of its popularity. New musical hits were arriving week by week, a surprising percentage of which were to linger on and become standards. All classes were taken to the auditorium one day to hear a one hour concert of band music by John Phillip Sousa and his band. What a showman he was, this little, white-haired, old man, standing to the side of the stage, with only his baton keeping time. Somehow keeping perfect precision, members featured in a portion of the marches would arrive front stage to play their part. When the trombones came front, playing the last strains of "Stars and Stripes Forever" very loud, the audience rose in a body without forethought. The music literally lifted them out of their seats.

I never had quite enough money to cover my expenses, week by week, and I didn't have enough to get my clothes laundered. By Friday my weekly allowance of eight dollars was spent. The landlady would lend me two dollars and fifty cents for the round trip home on the train so my clothes could be washed and pressed, and I could get eight dollars more. It went on that way throughout my first year at Hibbing. Every Sunday I'd pay the landlady for her loan and borrow it again on Friday.

Father told me at the end of the first college year that I would have to get a part-time job to cover my expenses, but Mother decided to cover expenses out of her fund from selling milk to customers. I was grateful, as keeping up with advanced students in chemistry and French would have been just that more difficult if not impossible. I changed rooming houses for the second year, and then in March 1929, a friend named Uno Ahlenius offered to let me room with him for free, which helped a great deal. There was then money for graduation pictures, but I could not afford the diploma, so I went through graduation exercises receiving a "dummy diploma," one made out to someone else who didn't graduate. Soon after Father informed me that he could not continue to finance my education, so I sought a job to save money for it on my own. I found employment almost immediately, as a clerk for the Interstate Iron Mining Company in their office at Carson Lake, a few miles west of Hibbing. The mine was an underground operation employing about two hundred men. It was named the South Agnew Mine. My work included keeping the payroll and dispensing supplies for the miners. Not owning an automobile, I travelled to and from work on a local bus. My wages were one hundred dollars per month. Transportation on the bus cost ten dollars a month. Our miners were earning about two hundred and fifty dollars a month, so I didn't feel well paid even as a new employee. What with paying for a room, buying meals, and clothing, it was impossible for me to save enough for continued studies in college, and there was no advanced school beyond the junior college in Hibbing. But I worked in the mine office for a year, becoming quite adept at putting out the payroll. Upon asking for a raise, I was granted one of ten dollars per month. That at least paid for my transportation to work, but I knew it was not enough to solve the problem of getting back to college. I began to think of other possibilities for attaining my goal.

BOOK IV

CHAPTER I

The Great Depression

Times were good in much of nineteen twenty-nine through-out the country. Iron ore was in great demand. It was said the iron range deposits would last for seventy-five to one hundred years. Jobs were still plentiful. True, the farmers got quite low prices for their produce, but they had been getting low prices since nineteen twenty-two. They raised food for their tables and ate well, though little cash was realized from crops. Population in the United States had reached one hundred and thirty million. Even at this level, forests in the Midwest were being used up at an alarming rate, but no one seemed too concerned.

The stock market crash in late nineteen twenty-nine had little effect on the great majority of people at first. They didn't own any stock. Items in the news media told of suicides by shooting or jumping out of windows. Actually there were very few. Another story told of men who had lost their fortunes selling apples in the streets. Again there may have been a few, but very few. Newsmen in later years love to dwell on these stories. The facts are that, no, the streets were not littered with the bodies of suicides, and no, not many people took to selling apples in the streets. For much of the year, apples would have frozen in the streets of northern cities. It wasn't until June of nineteen thirty that the job market began to tighten. The term "depression" had not, as yet, come into use. Most people felt that the economic slowdown was only tempo-rary, that business would get going again in a few months. Little did we know then how bad it would get!

Hearing rumors of good jobs at the steel mills in Chicago and the auto factories of Detroit, I decided to quit my job, move to a larger city to work, meanwhile carrying on with my education.

Mr. Tillinghast, the superintendent of the South Agnew mine was surprised when I told him of my plans to leave the company. He asked if I would stay for three months and train a replacement for my position, and I agreed to this arrangement. The training period passed swiftly, and as I left, Mr. Tillinghast said, "When you get back from Detroit, bring us the keys to the city." I guess that was meant to be sarcasm. He had a Bostonian accent, and his monthly salary was five hundred dollars. Five times the salary I received! For this amount he no doubt was depended on to keep the operation on a tight budget.

A former roommate and I were about to start for Detroit when we learned that a Hibbing man was leaving for Chicago soon in a Model T Ford. We decided to wait and travel with him, sharing expenses. It was almost a month before we finally got started. The driver decided to go to Chicago via Cedar Falls, Iowa. When we got to Cedar Falls, he suddenly discovered that he needed a new set of brakes so we had to stay over while they were repaired.

He also split the cost of the repairs three ways. Staying over at Cedar Falls plus the repair costs cut into our available funds. Then he wanted to stop at Galena, Illinois, to see former President Grant's home, losing more precious time.

Arriving in Chicago, we found living quarters. Unfortunately, they were so close to the elevated railway that the frequent passage of trains kept us awake most of the night. We decided to look for work while we were in Chicago. It didn't take us lone to find that jobs were indeed scarce. Several days of hunting yielded no work of any kind. Finally my former roommate landed a job at a steel mill, but I was unable to get work there. My funds were dwindling. I became discouraged. After a few more days of job hunting, I decided to return home to Meadowlands to wait for better times. My roommate wanted my new work clothing and my alarm clock, so I sold them to him. There was just enough money for the return trip. We all waited for working conditions throughout the states to improve, but gradually they got worse. Mining and automobile manufacture ceased entirely. A few banks and some insurance companies failed. Across the whole country, businesses either folded or cut back to austere, skeletal operations. Farm prices dropped further, and banks began to foreclose on mortgages. Father was fortunate. He had paid off the mortgage on his land. Besides, his position as road foreman for the St. Louis County highway department was secure. Roads were a necessity, and keeping them maintained was essential.

Soon after I returned to Meadowlands, Donald graduated from high school, and he enrolled in Hibbing Junior College, his expenses being defrayed by milk sales to customers in town. Sister Margie began to take over the milk route, carrying milk by hand. I did much of the farm chores, planting, harvesting, and helping Mother with gathering vegetables for canning. We raised some hogs and a steer for butchering each fall. We cured hams and bacon with smoke salt and let some of the meat freeze. Usually it stayed frozen solid all winter. But one winter we butchered a steer, and then the weather turned mild. The meat would not freeze. When it became evident that the carcass would spoil unless something was done to save it, we cut it up, and Mother canned the whole steer. What a job!

We never lacked for good food. Our garden was large. There was always plenty of fresh vegetables, corn, strawberries, and fruit in summer, and we canned preserved, dried, and stored for winter. From the standpoint of having plenty for our table, the Depression did not deprive us. It was of benefit to Father that I returned home. With Donald away in school, continuing help was needed to run the farm. The dairy herd had increased to twelve cows plus other animals, and it would have been hard for Father and Mother to manage the place while he worked on the county road job. In a way, he was better off than before the Depression began. Meanwhile sister Lillian was busy teaching for the county school system, first at one school then at another. She would call for a ride from where the bus stopped in Canyon. We would go to meet her and bring her home. She always brought news of her activities, and we enjoyed her company, and on Sunday evening we would take her back to her school or to her bus connection. We settled into the depressed times, and the years moved by.

To cut back on the expense of buying gasoline for the tractor and machine repair, Father decided to return to horse power. When E. Z. Marks came to town with another herd of horses, we went to the horse auction corral by the railroad, and Father purchased a fine looking team of western broncos.

He bought new sets of harness for them, and they were something to look at. But before long we found that one of them was unmanageable. I suspect that it had been used as a bucking horse at rodeos. Try as we would, we couldn't get it to settle down. It bucked while being harnessed, and we had to be careful that it didn't run away while attached to farm implements. After about a year, the team and harness were sold. Later, we heard that the horse had run away, broken a leg, and had to be shot. We went back to using the tractor for farm work.

With the collapse of the railroad land sales and development project and the closing of the lumber mill, jobs became indeed scarce. People who needed work to help with land payments, taxes, machinery purchases, gasoline, and clothing were in desperate straits. Individual logging operations were started to provide supplementary cash.

There were not more than a dozen steady year round jobs in the area, and they were occupied. The school faculty was imported entirely from other localities. The superintendent, principal, and coach were, as always, male, the teachers female. If a woman teacher got married, she automatically lost her job. The custom was so firmly established that it was never challenged.

There were not more than five privately owned businesses providing a living for the owners' families. It was necessary for farmers, who comprised the great majority of inhabitants, to cut their living expenses drastically and to gain almost all of their sustenance directly from the land. But there were household and farming items which were essential that could not be produced on a farm. Farmers were hard pressed for the wherewithal to purchase these necessary items.

107

Each winter, Father would supervise road graveling projects for the county road department. He had to be careful to see that a few weeks of work was allocated evenly among people wanting work. They were quick about complaining if one got more work than someone else.

There were also families living in the area who were not farmers, and others who had only a few acres and a cow. They could not possibly provide for themselves by farming. It was necessary for the government to provide sustenance for them, and so the first of the government aid programs was started. It was called, simply, Relief. The government bought surplus produce from farmers and distributed it to the indigent, usually through local grocery stores. Such items as pork, dried beans, flour, and other common staples were distributed. People who were too proud to accept these handouts, at first, soon changed their minds.

The Schleinitz family, owners of the former Hansen and Palmer store, told of a stout matron, mother of eight children, who came to the store and loudly maintained that she would never accept charity. Yet a few months later she was back demanding her share.

It soon became evident that simply waiting for the Depression to end would never bring it about. President Roosevelt had managed to save the monied interests, but that did nothing for the purchasing power of the masses. Regardless of the fact that demand for products of all kinds was greater than ever, people simply didn't have the exchange, the money, to buy. The Liberal faction, temporarily in power in Washington, D. C., advised Congress and the President to establish work projects nationwide to pump a little money down to the most needy, hoping to start it circulating and to require the recipients to work for it. The project was called the WPA, for Works Progress Administration. Work projects of all kinds proliferated throughout the country.

In Meadowlands a new sewer project was completed. Wages amounted to about sixty dollars a month. But to qualify for the work, a man had to be married, have children, and usually be on the Relief rolls. Some of the WPA employees were in need and deserving of the employment. However, on the WPA projects were some never do wells, drunks, and lazy men who qualified because they were what they were. They would laugh at industrious people, as they leaned on a shovel and talked. Much of their time was spent trudging to the latrine. However, in time, projects were completed. But the program left a bad taste in the mouths of industrious people who also needed work but who could not qualify, especially young, unmarried men who were excluded entirely from the work projects. WPA was obviously insufficient to prime the money circulation pump. More stimulus was needed.

The next government program to be launched was called PWA, for Public Works Administration. Unlike the WPA which was wholly subsidized by the Federal Government, PWA required communities to provide materials for construction projects, with help from the states. Many schools and other projects were built under this program. Wages were about the same as WPA, but the hours worked per week were limited. Jobs were available to family men or heads of households, as far as employees were needed, but this did not cover one-fourth of those who wanted to work. Once again young single folk were excluded from employment. They were indeed a lost, forgotten generation. A man asked me once, "What do you want a job for; you've got a place to stay and plenty to eat?" I realized that he was arguing for his own benefit. He didn't want to face the fact that I too might want a life of my own in the world.

The WPA kept some workers busy. But as time went by it became obvious that the country's money pump was not being primed. Massive amounts of cash were needed to start it flowing. They were not forthcoming. There were supposed to be brilliant people in Washington, D. C., advising the government. Did they not understand as any farmer does that to prime a pump it is necessary to pour at least half a bucket of water into it; that a dipper full just wouldn't do? Franklin Roosevelt, by his speeches, indicated a liberal approach. But he was no traitor to his class. Eventually, we would rise speedily out of the Depression, but not because of government programs. Long before World War II began, the powers that govern had chosen sides and started furnishing their favorites with arms as they did in the first World War. We would wait a while for the spark which would plunge us into war, but that gets ahead of my story.

The next program to surface was the CCC or Civilian Conservation Corps. Now, at last, the government was going to do something for the young men and women of the country, we thought. The new program was advertised as employment for the young, to teach them new skills, meanwhile taking them off of the backs of their parents, and feeding and housing them. It sounded good. They were to get thirty dollars a month, along with room and board during the training period. As soon as the program got under way the restrictions became evident. Only men whose parents were on relief, or on public programs were eligible.

Single persons living with parents who were employed, or not on programs for indigents, were again excluded. Those who were accepted were required to sign over a portion of their pay, usually half, to their parents. A few trips to town, a movie, cigarettes, and maybe an evening or two spent at neighborhood dances would take care of the remaining fifteen dollars. For training, most of the CCC boys spent their time trimming brush and the lower branches from trees along highways throughout the country, something that one can learn in an hour. How many would use this skill later to earn a living? They were housed in bunkhouses and fed in cookshacks, lumberjack fashion. It is probable that the CCC program was really a ploy to get young men off of the streets of our towns and cities where they might have started making trouble.

For young men and women living with non-indigent, industrious parents, it was another promise offered and then snatched away.

State Employment agencies were set up in most cities of the United States. They would send representatives out to rural communities once a week to take applications of job seekers for work. These applications were valid for only a limited time and required renewal to remain in effect. Week after week, we young unemployed folk would journey to Floodwood to see our job representative and talk over prospects for employment. The result, no work. Finally, in the winter of 1934, I asked the employment representative what my prospects were, being young, single, and living at home with my parents. He replied that my prospects were nil, and that my hope was to "Dig out," that is, to go somewhere else. As I rode home, I asked myself, "Dig out? To where?"

Looking back about forty years, after having witnessed the marches, protests, and violence resorted to by young people and against them during the Vietnam War, I have pondered the question of why youth during the Great Depression did not express themselves in like fashion. Surely our plight was much more aggravating to us, and it covered a period of about ten years. I can only vouchsafe my opinion. First, we lived in a rural setting, and it would have done little good to march around among one's neighbors in a small town. Second, President Roosevelt was an inspiring and sympathic speaker. We hung on his every word, and our hopes were rekindled again and again. In the end he failed to raise the Depression except by war. Recently, a general was quoted as saying, "There isn't anything wrong with this country that a good war couldn't cure."' That is about the same as saying that if our country is to be prosperous, all we have to do is to start a war and kill people. How foreigners must love us if they think we really believe that. Such are some of our leaders.

Third, and last, many young people of the Depression years had parents of foreign upbringing. Obedience by children to their parents was the rule in Europe. Our parents, knowingly or not, brought their European, patriarchal ideas with them and raised us in their image. We would do nothing to embarrass them publicly, or endanger their jobs, or their citizenship.

Of course, the Depression, had no war intervened, could not have gone on indefinitely. There would certainly have been a major political upheaval. But the war did intervene, so we do not know what would have happened. The answer to this riddle may be in our future.

One hot summer afternoon in July, nineteen hundred and

thirty-three we were standing by our windmill on the farm drinking some water, when we chanced to look westward. What appeared to be a grey-black wall or curtain covered the western sky from north to south. It stood from high in the sky down to tree level, and it was rapidly moving in our direction. Then it was upon us, the first of the Dakota Dust Bowl storms to reach northern Minnesota. Daylight darkened to a dusty, gritty twilight. We decided to stop working for the day and went home. During the night, the dust storm gradually abated though the particles kept settling to earth for several days. Fortunately for us, the area in which we lived was well covered with forests and other vegetation, so none of our soil blew away. In fact we gained some, and subsequent rains anchored it to the native earth.

The reader may wonder if, during the Depression years, we just sat and waited for better times. Far from it. Unfortunately, in what may be called normal times, people spend few of their hours thinking or talking about their government. But as the Depression deepened a new interest in politics began to flourish. Arguments about government policies were held with no holds barred, wherever people chanced to meet.

Regardless of the times we were always busy. There were chores to be done, crops to plant, cultivate, and harvest, Depression or no.

Soon after President Roosevelt's inauguration, bankers, insurance men, and leaders of large financial organizations came to him, hat in hand, asking that they be saved from disaster. It became his first order of business to accommodate them. Protective measures were passed, and for the time they were satisfied. But when he instigated programs to help the average American, their gratitude changed to enmity, their friendship to hatred. They could not see beyond their own greedy nature, thinking only of self and money. What might have happened to them if no relief programs were instigated is hard to determine. But it is likely that they were saved by Roosevelt's programs in spite of themselves.

We forgot about coal and went back to wood for heating and cooking during the Depression. We did a lot of walking, especially in winter when cars were hard to start, carrying our milk cans or whatever had to be transported. We were out of doors much of the time. Our fuel, there, was food and lots of it. Mother loved to cook, and she was very good at it, so we were fortunate.

We read a lot, and books were always available for winter evenings. Sanders Olson, a nearby farmer, owned a complete set of Dickens. I waded through the whole set, borrowing one book at a time.

Three times a week, summer evenings, we practiced playing baseball, and there were games regularly on Sunday afternoons. Father often wanted us to work evenings with him on the farm after his day of work for the county, but usually our game practice intervened and he didn't insist. Our manager was his truck driver for the county. Our small country area entered the Iron Range baseball league and gained considerable attention. With a population of about five hundred, including farmers, our team played Range teams on fairly even terms, though their populations ranged from three thousand to fifteen thousand. More important, it gave us something to do and think about during those years.

There was a program sponsored by the government to preserve the theater and the arts. Theatrical groups were formed, subsidized partly by a federal program, partly by business, and partly by the sale of tickets. A group called the Kahler players was formed in Duluth, and they toured nearby small towns once or twice a month to put on their plays. They were excellent actors, and their productions were well selected. The comedies were hilarious, and our town hall was packed with people whenever they performed. Admission at the door was a quarter. This entertainment was usually far superior to what has been projected on television in recent years, and for a tiny fraction of the cost.

During the fall wild game seasons, we hunted deer and game birds. One is tempted to start off with a host of deer hunting stories. But they probably would only be of interest to enthusiasts, so they will be omitted. Let it suffice to say that while we enjoyed hunting, we were primarily meat hunters. To us it was part of the harvest cycle.

On Saturday evenings, there was usually a dance, either in Meadowlands or in a neighboring community. A group of four of us usually congregated at the village tavern where Ted Langren would pick us up in his Chrysler. He was the only one of us who owned a car, and he was always willing to provide transportation. We didn't take girls with us. We couldn't afford to. But usually there were as many girls at the dances as there were men. The dances were enjoyable highlights of the week. But if romances budded at these gatherings, they usually died on the vine. There was no way out for the unemployed young folk. A tendency developed to avoid any serious entanglements, to treat all situations lightly. But beneath it all lurked an unspeakable bitterness.

Our family attended church only on religious holidays, when special programs were scheduled. Mother seldom attended, and Father never. He was an agnostic until his last few years.

Evenings, we often tuned in radio music of one or another of the dance bands then popular throughout the country, such as Ted Weems, Tommy Dorsey, or Harry James. To read a book while enjoying their music was one of our favorite pastimes. Most of the great bands are no longer in existence. A few orchestras of that era continue to the present day on television, but they were not among the very popular ones of the thirties.

Every small town had a movie theater, and finances permitting, we would occasionally go to see a motion picture show. Hollywood producers were obsessed by two hang-ups in producing motion pictures. Their first objective was to provide a few hours of escape for movie patrons from the despair brought on by the Depression. One could watch a movie and for a short time, live a vicarious, splendid, dream. How much better would it have been for the people if the shows had been devoted to the depression dilemma, pointing to possible solutions to their plight. Except for one show, The Grapes of Wrath, which portrayed stark realities of the times, no social documentary films were produced.

The second hang-up was that bigger is better. Why have three or four good dancers in the chorus line when you could put a hundred on the stage? There was a song referring to a "thousand violins." Fortunately there was never enough room on the stage for that many violins. Most shows of the thirties could be referred to as spectacles. You left the theater knowing you had seen a lot of something, but you were never quite sure what it was.

Occasionally a comical news exchange would take place between the "Hayes Office" which was supposed to oversee morality in pictures, and the Catholic Church. Church officials would attack film productions, saying they were uncensored and immoral. Before very long, the Hollywood producers would make a movie of a religious story, starring a priest who was by far the greatest of all the saints. After that, no more was heard from the Church. Motion picture production continued, perhaps a bit more immoral than before.

CHAPTER II

Jobs in the Depression

Occasionally we were invited to neighbors' homes, or they would come to ours for holiday feasts. The food that the women-folk could prepare for these events from home grown produce was something for chefs to envy.

In the spring of nineteen hundred and thirty-four, Uncle Fred was temporarily laid off from his job of locomotive engineer. He came to live with us again, occupying the second floor of our home. He decided that he was going to raise ten acres of oats on his forty acres that we were also using for cattle pasture. He made arrangements with Father to borrow the tractor, plow, disc, and seeder to prepare and seed the land and he staked it out for cultivation. I brought the tractor and plow to the designated area and plowed the first furrow each way to help him get started. I had just completed the furrows when Fred came walking up-with his engineer's garb and cap on. I gave him some brief instructions about steering and operating the tractor. Steering was easy as one had only to keep the right front wheel in the last furrow, with a slight crank leftwards, and the tractor would practically steer itself. He took the wheel, started plowing, and I headed home-wards. In a few minutes I glanced back to see how he was progressing. To my amazement, he was going in a circle, heading for the woods. I ran back, and when I reached the tractor, he stopped it and walked toward home stomping and swearing. Watching him, I finally deduced the reason for his failure to operate the tractor. He had been operating a railroad locomotive for about twenty years, and one does not have to steer a locomotive. He had never owned or operated an automobile.

I got on the tractor, plowed, disked, and seeded the land using Father's seed oats. That fall we harvested the crop and sold it with our own. We wondered whether we should bring up the subject again to Fred. Finally, we never mentioned it. We didn't want to embarrass him, or worse yet, bring on another bout of stomping and swearing.

In June of nineteen hundred and thirty-five, I travelled by bus to California. If this is an unexpected surprise to the reader, let him be assured it was as much of a surprise to me. It came about in this manner.

My brother Axel had completed a six year stint in the United States Navy. During his enlistment he had learned the trade of first class machinist. After leaving the Na-vy he went to call on "Uncle Andy Anderson" at El Segundo, the same man who had sheltered Father when he had first arrived in Chicago from Sweden. Andy, now a retired boilermaker and living near the E1 Segundo refinery, gave Axel a friendly reception and through acquaintances at Standard Oil placed him in a steady job as a machinist for that company.

In his next letter, Axel told us of his good fortune, and he requested that I come to stay with him and try for work at Standard Oil. I was only too happy to get started. Having very limited funds after purchasing my bus ticket, it was necessary for me to travel continuously, except for rest and meal interruptions. The trip lasted for three days and four nights. It was my first long trip on a bus. The motion of the vehicle and its throbbing engine kept me awake day and night for the entire trip, except once when I slept for one hour of the eighty-four which it took to reach Los Angeles. I have since learned that keeping awake so long can be dangerous. As we traveled through the last mountain ranges of California, strange sensations occurred. It would seem that the bus was going uphill where it was really going downhill. There was a lack of coordination between what my eyes saw and what my other senses told me.

117

The Los Angeles bus depot was located in the foyer of a hotel. As I stepped from the bus with my suitcase, the thought kept running through my mind that it was time to milk the cows, and I must hurry and get at it. Yet I knew the thought was nonsense.

Registering quickly in the hotel, I hurried to my room, undressed, and fell into bed. Sleep came almost instantly. By the next morning I was completely rested and refreshed.

When Axel received my phone call, he contacted a friend who had an automobile, and they drove to the hotel to pick me up. Soon we were at the house where we were to stay together for over a year. I was surprised to find that Axel, who loved automobiles, did not have one. He had always owned a car of one make or another before. But here he lived only about four blocks from the Standard Oil entry gate, so it was no problem for him to get to work.

I began a concentrated effort to get a job with Standard Oil, the only manufacturing firm in El Segundo. Morning after morning, for several months I would go to the employment office hoping to get work, but I found they were either not hiring or would only hire back former employees. Finally, I was taken on for three weeks' periods when the distillery plants needed cleaning. I searched the town for other employment but to no avail. The situation was similar all over the country. The Navy had so many applicants that one would have to wait six months after enlistment to begin service, at twenty-five dollars per month.

We lived in a small house on Grand Avenue, a few doors from the sand hills that stretched westward to the Pacific Ocean beach. I began to cook our meals, wash our clothes, and clean the house, in between periods of employment.

Hearing that men were being hired at Columbia Steel Corporation in Torrance twenty miles away, I quickly caught a ride to apply and was hired as a floorman for an overhead crane. The pay was thirty-eight cents an hour, the minimum allowed by the National Recovery Act, the NRA, three dollars and four cents per day. I found lodging in a rooming house and ate my meals at a family style boarding house across the street. After paying for my room and board, there was enough left over for haircuts, new work clothing and miscellaneous necessities. I tried for an advanced position but without success. When I had worked at Columbia Steel for about two months, steel orders declined, and work was reduced to four days per week. Checking on the reduction in pay, I found that I would be donating my clothing, haircuts, and miscellaneous necessities to the company in order to work for them. I therefore quit my job and returned to El Segundo to live with Axel and resume periodic employment with Standard Oil. Between jobs, when the housework was completed, I would walk southward and spend a few hours swimming or sunning myself at Manhattan, Hermosa, or Redondo Beaches.

Friends took me along with them on a trip over the "Ridge Route" to the San Juaqin Valley. We stopped at Arvin, then made a tour in the Bakersfield area. They pointed out a desolate uncultivated area known as the Weed Patch. I ran into that name later in John Steinbeck's Grapes of Wrath. The housing area for the "Okies" that he described was not there. He must have chosen that name so as not to identify it with any particular town or locality.

Occasionally, Axel and I were invited over to "Uncle Andy's" for dinner. Before the meal he always served us a half glass of straight whiskey, topped off with a bottle of beer, a "boilermaker." He was a fine old gentleman, and his housekeeper, Emma Fox was an excellent cook.

One of Axel's friends, "Red" Manson, had gotten a job as a welder up in the oil fields near Taft. Red's wife, Kate, was one of the Duley girls. There were five girls in the family. The four sisters of Kate decided to drive up to visit with her. They took me along to take care of car trouble, especially for changing tires if it was necessary. The sister who drove was good at it, but a fast driver. We travelled at about eighty miles an hour most of the way. There were no flat tires. If there had been, I wondered if there would have been any need to change them. But we got back without problems.

It is better that I leave out names on this next occasion. It was Thanksgiving Day, and Axel had to work. He told me before leaving, not to make my meal at home, but to buy Thanksgiving dinner at a restaurant. I did so and arrived back at the house about twelve fifteen. I had scarcely gotten home when a car pulled up outside. It carried a couple of fellows who were Axel's friends. Their wives had gotten together and prepared a bounteous Thanksgiving dinner. Knowing that I was home alone, they had sent their husbands to bring me to eat with them. I told them that I had already eaten, but they insisted that I come, regardless. Seeing that there was no way I could avoid it, I went, hoping to take small servings and just taste the food. The fellows had been drinking. They had acquired some alcohol and rock candy and had proceeded to make some liquor that they called "Rock and Rye." We arrived shortly at the home where the festivities were to be held. Upon our arrival the ladies began to dish up bowls and platters of food. But the two men kept running outside for another drink. They were in bad shape when we finally sat down to dinner. We had no sooner started eating when one of the men fell asleep with his face among the potatoes, gravy, and turkey on his plate. His wife was boiling angry, but she preserved her dignity, raised his head up, and wiped the food off of his face. She took the plate away and brought him a piece of pie on another plate. He promptly picked up his fork and began to chop away at the pie. It was too much for his wife. She picked up the pie plate and slapped it squarely in his face. Pie flew on the drapes, the table, clothing, 211 over the area. I tried to maintain a poker face, ate sparingly, and praised the food. I felt sorry for the wives, how embarrassed they must have felt. As soon as I could tactfully do so, I thanked them profusely, and making my escape, walked home.

Axel was never one to do a good job of handling his finances. For a time he would perform the function well. Then, when one least expected it, he would draw his paycheck, catch a bus, and head for San Diego. He would return in a couple of days with only pennies in his pocket. There would follow a period of buying on credit, meanwhile stalling on the paying of bills until he was back on his feet again. It must have been the Navy life that had made him that way.

We continued to subsist, but I was ambitious about getting ahead, and it seemed that I was once again up against a stone wall. At the end of one and one-half years, I decided to return to Minnesota. I was 27 years old. Acknowledging defeat in California, I boarded the bus for Duluth, Minnesota, and was soon back on the farm. My brother Donald had gone as far with his education as Hibbing Junior College would allow and had found part-time work in a school laboratory at the University of Minnesota while taking a few college courses in his spare time. Lillian had moved from her teaching position with the St. Louis County Schools to the Chisholm High School System.

It seemed someone was always opposing Bill Newman, Father's supervisor, the county commissioner, for election. With jobs so scarce it was easy for aspirants for road jobs to join with opponents of the administration in office. Finally, in the election of nineteen thirty-six, with Mister Newman facing formidable opposition, Father resigned from his road foreman's position and henceforth gave his full attention to farming.

It became evident that living at the house in town while working on the farm in the country was an unhandy situation and changes would have to be made. A new barn had been built on high ground south of town, so plans were started to erect a home near it. Father bought a small dwelling and moved it from the site where a county road shop would later be constructed, to the farmyard, where it remained for several years before it could be placed over a concrete basement and remodeled with added rooms.

When the new barn was built, it was necessary for us to have a new well drilled not far from it. We had heard that John Lofgren, an old bachelor from out in the country, was one of those gifted in the art of water witching.

We asked him to come to the farm one evening to practice his craft and find a suitable location for the well. He arrived on schedule with his forked willow wand. Father pointed out the location near where we hoped to find water, and taking one branch of the forked stick in each hand, John went to work. Before long it became evident that he was quite drunk. He went staggering around the area while we almost burst trying to restrain our laughter. At length the forked stick bent downwards. John tried the spot from all directions. Every time, the stick bent down the same way at the same place. Finally he said "Dig here," and we marked where he indicated. Later we drilled the well and found that John had found an abundant supply of clear, cold water about fifty-four feet beneath the surface. It appeared that his condition didn't hinder his water witching one bit.

In the spring of nineteen thirty-seven word came that the automobile factories were hiring men in Detroit. We wasted no time.

Ted Landgren owned a good automobile, and he was anxious to get started. Beside him there were Maynard Speece, Russell Johnson and myself as passengers. We stopped overnight with Steve Roth in Chicago and arrived in Detroit the following day. Quickly, we rented the upstairs of a private home in Highland Park, moved in, and were ready to look for work the following morning.

Our landlord informed us that Murray Corporation, a maker of Ford car bodies, was hiring men, so we hurried to apply for work at that factory. To our amazement and joy we were hired that day, along with about ten thousand other men. The wage was ninety cents per hour. It seemed that our job quest was over. The following Sunday we decided to celebrate by going somewhere for a big dinner. There was a Finnish restaurant near our apartment that advertised chicken dinners, all one could eat for one dollar. The amount of food we ate that day was tremendous. We were uncomfortable for some time afterward. Three weeks later, we, along with the other ten thousand men hired by Murray, were laid off.

We soon learned that large factories were inclined to work at full capacity until a quota of work was completed, and then they would shut down. There was no such thing as a skeletal or reduced operation.

Hearing of our plight, the landlord told us that his brother-in-law was foreman for a conveyor construction company, and we might go to the hiring hall to try for work there. Meanwhile he contacted the relative, and we were all hired again, this time to construct, repair, or reroute all types of conveyors. We covered most of the auto factories in Detroit. There were small contracts lasting only one day, others lasting as long as three weeks.

We contacted Sarah Orr, who had formerly taught with my sister Lillian at Homecroft. She and her Husband Sandy, an electrician, entertained us for dinner, and later we took them out to a night club for another meal. Sandy was engaged at the time installing the electrical wiring on a new lake ship for Henry Ford. When the boat was ready to be launched, he took us to the launching site to watch. As we looked on, Henry Ford, Sr., walked by, leading a little girl by the hand. They climbed into a small viewing stand. The ropes were cut, and the ship slid sidewise into the lake.

In about two months all of the conveyor work was completed. Automobile companies commenced operating again, using only men with much seniority. Once again we were out of work and headed back to Meadowlands. In nineteen thirty-eight we four made another trip to Detroit. It was a repeat performance of the previous year, about three months of work and a return home. Time was slipping by. December the first of nineteen thirty-eight brought with it my twenty-ninth birthday.

CHAPTER III

Back to College

In March of nineteen thirty-nine, Lillian offered to lend me the money to complete my education. It did not take long for me to accept. I enrolled at Duluth Teachers' College in time for the spring quarter and found a room in the men's dormitory nearby. Having been out of school for ten years, I found at first, that I could not seem to concentrate upon studies outside of class for more than ten minutes at a time. "So be it," I thought. I would walk around a bit, anything to relax, and then return to work. Gradually my powers of concentration lengthened until I was able to continue working for four hours at a stretch. That was enough. A couple of four hour sessions of study per day would do, and I would hold to that until graduation.

It was wonderful to be back in school. After so many years of frustration, it felt good to be on the move, to-be progressing steadily toward a goal once more. I would work hard and guard my opportunity carefully.

Near the end of the first spring quarter, Doctor Corfield, The Dean of Men , called me into his office for a chat. He questioned me about my work and travels and told me about his own doctorate project of studying sponges in the Caribbean Sea. I enjoyed our visit, wondering on the side, what this somewhat pudgy, middle-aged bachelor had in mind. I was soon to learn why. The present student manager of the men's dormitory was to graduate at quarter's end, and a search was on for a mature person to take his place. A few days later, Doctor Sorenson, president of the college, called me to his office. After our greetings, the first thing he did was to ask me to write my name on a pad of paper which he offered. I complied and he took the pad. He scrutinized my writing thoroughly, then asked if I would take over management of the men's dormitory. I accepted, of course, as it meant that I would receive my room and board free. There are people who strive to analyze character by handwriting, and I suppose he was one of them.

As Manager of the dormitory, I was expected to be in residence for the regular school year and for the two summer sessions as well. I could study while supervising up to twenty-seven young men residing at Washburn Hall. We took all of our meals in the basement dining room of the women's dorm, along with the women residents. The college, with an enrollment of about seven hundred and fifty students, was an efficiently operated little community, a university in miniature. Its curriculum was limited to the various teaching arts. But there was a feeling of camaraderie, a kinship which larger schools can never attain. I began to feel a peace and serenity of mind which had been absent for a long time. The dormitory supervisory work meant that I would have to borrow much less from Lillian during my time in school, in all eight hundred and eighty-four dollars, which I would return in full during the following three years.

Inasmuch as my presence was required winter and summer, it seemed advisable to add an Industrial Arts major to the English major already in progress, so this was accomplished.

It is a pleasure to remember brilliant professors of English such as Saltus and Sandin; for history, Pieper. The music department was excellent and very active. Each year there would be a week long seminar. A prominent musician would perform several concerts and would meet with students for sessions daily. It happened that the job of seeing to the musician guests' comforts and escorting them to meals, etc., fell to me, as they were usually lodged in the men's dormitory. Thus I got to meet Roland Hayes, the black singer, also a member of the Chicago Opera, and Sigmund Spaeth, a concert pianist who was called '"the tune detective." Mr. Spaeth was often called when there was a lawsuit, to determine whether or not one composer had stolen another's tune.

While at the dormitory, I came in contact with another government program, the National Youth Administration (NYA). It seemed, the government had finally decided to offer aid to needy students in school by subsidizing the menial tasks which they could perform. Several student workers were placed under my supervision for janitorial duties. Other needy students chose to join the National Guard for once a week drill sessions, to earn a little money for expenses. Needless to say, when the military build-up commenced, these were the first men to be called to army camps, even before they had completed school and before war against anyone had been declared. Japan, anxious to expand, would eventually light the fuse.

Scholarships as such, were nonexistent at Duluth State Teachers' College at the time, but a few students were employed as lab assistants on a part-time basis.

In July, nineteen forty-one, I graduated with a Bachelor of Science degree. Several months previous to this time we prospective graduates had been sending out applications for teaching positions. As teacher hiring usually happens in March, we were not at all sure that jobs would be available. Civil Service wanted a registry of applicants to be utilized later for instructing Army Air Corps mechanics. Application blanks were distributed by the head instructor of our Industrial Arts Department. Most of the Industrial Arts graduates signed up as a hedge against lack of teaching jobs.

After graduation I went home to Meadowlands to help Father and Mother complete their house on the farm and to aid them in moving their furniture and household equipment. They were getting older, and living closer to the farm operation would ease their labors somewhat. Late one fall afternoon, we roamed through the house in town to see if we had forgotten to load anything onto the truck before leaving. We were tired. Mother said that she didn't really want to move to the farm. She had raised her family in the older home, and she would remember it with love as the real

126

home of her active years. Hurriedly, we helped her into the truck seat beside the driver and started with our load to the farm house. The transition was made without a show of emotion, but underneath we knew it was the end of one era of our lives.

It seems in order to do a roll call of our relatives to see what happened to them throughout the Depression years. Aunt Ida and Uncle Hans had moved about 1930 from Keewatin to a farm outside of Cook, Minnesota, where they began raising cows and chickens. Hans had tired of his job as captain in an underground mine. The farm was located about three blocks from the western tip of Lake Vermillion. It was pretty much a wilderness area then. Sometimes on a winter evening, they would start out and walk to a neighbor's house three miles away for a visit.

Their son, John Victor, would eventually graduate as a dentist from the University of Minnesota and would make a career of Oral Reconstructive Surgery in the United States Navy, retiring as a Captain to live with his wife, Mary, in Hawaii.

Aunt Sandra and her husband August were doing well in their farming and logging operations at Gheen, Minnesota. They raised two sons who would later graduate from the University of Minnesota. Bruno became a medical doctor in the United States Navy, while Wilho made a career of teaching at the University.

Uncle Frank Maki meanwhile had an engineer's position at a box factory in Tower, Minnesota. Together with the factory superintendent, he owned a cabin on the eastern shore of Whitefish Bay, north of Lake Vermillion. Being familiar with the area, he knew about the best deer habitat and the best places to fish. I was invited to fish with him several times, and once, for a hunting trip. I have promised not to tell hunting stories, but I cannot keep from describing a remarkable shot he made on that hunting expedition. There were six of us, three scattered along a ridge and three driving the deer across our position. It appeared that we had not flushed even one deer, so we gathered on the high ridge to reconnoiter. Far below us, Frank spied a big doe that had somehow slipped around us without being seen. It was about a half mile away, threading its way along a trail in the valley. Frank looked at his gun, a thirty-ought six bolt action. The distance was too far to make an accurate shot with it. The old man who had come with us mainly to do the cooking was carrying a Savage lever action of two hundred and fifty-three thousand caliber, a powerful gun. Frank borrowed it and with a standing shot, knocked the deer staggering sideways. We were about to take our toboggan and start after the deer, but he said, "No, wait about five minutes; let the deer stiffen up and lay down." We followed his advice, though we were eager to get started. When we caught up with it, we found that it had indeed laid down not far from the place where it had been shot. It rose slowly and began to trot lamely away, but we brought it down, gutted it, and returned to the party. Later, Frank, while on another hunting foray became ill with spinal meningitis and died. I drove my mother to Tower for his funeral. Of his four children, only one, Lillian survives, living in Seattle, Washington.

About nineteen thirty-seven, Uncle Werner came down with tuberculosis. He was taken to the sanitarium at Nopeming where he lingered on, finally passing away at the age of fifty-three, in nineteen forty. We gathered at Meadowlands for the funeral. He was the first of Father's relatives not to be buried at Turtle Lake, Wisconsin. In time, his widow Edda would move with her children to Michigan where they now live, except for the oldest boy, Edgar Warner, who was killed in a hunting accident.

In nineteen forty a letter was received from brother Axel informing us that he had married for the second time and that he and his new wife, Katherine were living on a farm at McFarland not far from Bakersfield. Axel invited Margie to live at the farm and commute daily to the Junior College-at Bakersfield to complete her secretarial course. Previously, she had completed semesters at Duluth State Teachers' and Hibbing Junior College. She soon departed on her new venture to California.

After World War II, brother Axel moved from the farm at McFarland, to Delano, California, where he and a partner went into business, manufacturing farm equipment. His marriage to Katherine foundered, and he began going with Milan, a Swedish divorcee, whom he later married, and adopted her son, Ky.

Donald, somewhere in the same time span, had moved to California. He became disappointed with the job prospects there and moved to Richmond, Indiana, where he found employment and where he would marry Lelia Branson and raise five children, four boys and one girl. Their names are Charles, Phillip, Timothy, John, and Ann.

Sister Lillian grew weary of teaching in the early years after nineteen forty. She quit for about one year and took a job at an aircraft factory in Santa Monica. However, she soon tired of that work also and went back to teaching. She would marry twice in Los Angeles; first to George B. Vance, an Internal Revenue employee and second, to Viggo Danielson, a grain farmer from Poplar, Montana. Her teaching continued through most of this period.

In late August of nineteen forty-one, I received notification to apply as Industrial Arts instructor at the High School in St. Charles, Minnesota. I hurried there, was accepted, and began my teaching career. St. Charles was-a fine farming community of about twenty-five hundred people twenty miles east of Rochester, which is famous for its Mayo Clinic. I was responsible for teaching a wide range of shop crafts, and seven months went by quickly. I joined the Southwestern Minnesota Industrial Arts Association. March is the traditional rehiring time for teachers for the next year's term. At our February Association meeting we were advised to ask for forty-five dollars per month raises for the next term. One day in March, the school superintendent stopped in at the shop where I was tidying up after my day of instruction. He said, 1 lI was just going to ask what you might be expecting in the way of a raise for next year." I said, "Well, I was hoping for a raise of forty-five dollars. He said, "Are you serious?" I informed him of the Association's advice regarding raises. He said that he would talk it over with the board and left the room. My salary at the time was one hundred and thirty dollars per month. Hog prices were climbing sharply, and farmers were already making around fifteen thousand dollars per year. It is quite probable that the school board didn't yet realize what was already beginning to happen to wages in the country. They gave each teacher a ten dollar raise, but for me they offered twenty. They also added that If I could get the forty-five dollar raise somewhere else, to give them the chance to match it, so they could hold on to my services. I agreed on condition that if the government wanted me to teach aviation mechanics that I would be released. I was called to Rantoul, Illinois, to begin a short course in the teaching of aviation mechanics on April twenty-first and left St. Charles before the end of the high school term. By that fall the St. Charles school system would be paying two hundred dollars per month for an industrial arts teacher. It must have been a surprise to the superintendent and the board.

The teacher preparatory course at Chanute Field lasted for six months; the salary was one hundred and fifteen dollars per month, fifteen dollars less than my salary at St. Charles. But as soon as I started teaching aviation mechanics, I got a hefty raise. By the end of two years, I was making more than double my beginning salary at St. Charles. I was trying to make up for the lost years. Training completed, I was transferred to Lincoln, Nebraska, where, at the nearby airbase, my duties of training Army Air Corps mechanics began. Every extra dollar went to pay back the loan to Lillian. It was paid off just in time for what was to come.

CHAPTER IV

War and Romance

Uncle Sam, who had ignored young men of my circumstance during the ten years of the Depression, revealed that he knew where we were all along. I received my "Greetings" in late September with instructions to report at Duluth for induction into the Army on November the ninth of nineteen and forty-three. I would continue after basic training, to instruct aviation mechanics as before, but with my salary reduced from about two hundred and seventy-five dollars to sixty dollars plus meals, bunk, and uniforms. Making up for the lost years would have to wait a couple of years more.

In October of nineteen forty-three, I journeyed home to spend a few weeks with the folks in Meadowlands before reporting for induction. News from there had not been good. Father had not been feeling well. When he had a physical examination in nineteen forty-two, the doctor had told him that he had an enlarged heart, that he could go immediately, or he could live for ten years if he were careful. We, his sons and daughters, had tried to get him to sell off the livestock and just retire on the farm. He and Mother could raise a small garden if they wished, but we would all send money for their subsistence. Our suggestion was to no avail. The farming continued as before.

One day Ilo Johnson, a daughter of a neighboring family brought her friend the county nurse to the farm. She was Viola Tormondsen, formerly of Grand Marais, Minnesota, now stationed in Meadowlands. Viola and I were soon "going steady." Knowing how short the time was before I would have to enter the service, we decided to get married as soon as arrangements could be competed. The marriage was solemnized on November fourth at the home of Vi's Aunt Elizabeth Gilbertsen in Duluth. We spent our short honeymoon in a hotel. I was to leave on November the ninth with a bus load of other recruits, but a severe snow storm blocked all roads and we were granted two more days before I left for Fort Snelling. Induction completed, I was transferred to Buckley Field, twenty miles east of Denver about New Year's Day of nineteen forty-four. Viola decided to come to Denver to be near, so she moved into an apartment with a service couple and I would catch the bus as often as possible to be with her.

Buckley Field was an Army Air Corps basic training camp. Between January and April of nineteen forty-four, its personnel were ravaged by influenza. Many men were so hoarse, myself among them, that we could only talk in a whisper. Unable to talk, I would call my wife on the telephone and have a whispering conversation with her.

We left Denver for Fresno, California, the staging area, on April first and we remained there about one month while my new orders were prepared. Then it was on to Santa Rosa, California, where we found a small apartment in which to live. I commuted by bus each day through orchards and vineyards to the Air Corps pilot training field. Santa Rosa was to be our home for much of the time until I was released from service in nineteen forty-five. On October twenty-first of nineteen forty-four, our first child, Pauline, was born. Viola really had someone to keep her busy while I was at the air base. Her parents spent several months living in an apartment nearby before moving to San Diego.

It was not very long after our arrival that Germany surrendered, and war operations in Europe ceased. The war effort changed to the Pacific Area. With the bombing of Hiroshima and Nagasaki, war came to an end in that area as well, except for the occupation of enemy territory. For a time it appeared that I would go with the occupation forces, but in view of my age, I suppose, I was never sent.

The war over, servicemen were to be released in order of

length of service. Having less service time than many I had to wait until October thirty-first, nineteen forty-five for my discharge and received it at Sacramento on that date. Viola and Pauline had gone to San Diego, and I followed them there hoping to find work there, but jobs there were scarce, so we decided to return to Minnesota, arriving at Meadowlands about November twenty-first.

Within a week I would be thirty-six years old. We had no automobile. The job I held training aviation mechanics before entering service no longer existed. Thus we faced the future starting from scratch. War and the Depression had eaten away twelve of the fifteen years since my twenty-first birthday. Once again we would try to make up for the lost years.

Having been discharged on October thirty-first, I was too late for the usual teacher hiring period. Schools were already in session and all positions were filled. Industry was retooling for peacetime production but that would take considerable time. A large segment of discharged veterans were back on the street, unable to find work. The government provided a temporary weekly sum for veterans who applied, and who were unable to find employment. It was not enough for a veteran and his family to house, feed, and clothe themselves, so most of them moved in with relatives temporarily until work could be located. After drawing this stipend for several weeks, I located a job loading paper into box cars for a paper manufacturing company in Cloquet. In the meantime, searching for better and more meaningful employment, I applied to the Veterans Administration for a position as Training Officer in the new veteran's training programs. The G.I. Bill veteran's training program was soon launched, and under its financial aid and sponsorship, millions of veterans received, continued, or completed training at colleges, trades, or on the farm. It was spoken of as a magnanimous gesture to reward veterans for their years of service, and this was indeed true. For those of us who had already received our degrees, etc., often on borrowed money, it offered little except for a course of study now and then at summer school, covering tuition, books, and supplies.

The G.I. Bill had another objective not so well advertised.

133

Since all veterans would not be able to find work for some time, it would draw some of them out of the labor market for a few years. It would not do, might even be dangerous to have Depression-scarred, battle hardened men walking the streets for long. No doubt, along with the magnanimity, this feature was fully recognized by the power elite who ran the government.

I served in the capacity of training officer for the Veterans Administration for four and one-half years, working for six months in St. Paul and in Duluth and its environs for the remaining four years. As veterans completed their training or ran out of benefit time, the program diminished, and our positions were curtailed. I was laid off in nineteen fifty. There followed two years with the Duluth Public Schools instructing a class of problem boys. At the end of that time I took what I originally thought to be a summer job with the newly arrived Western Electric Company. I decided to remain with the company and eventually retired from my job with that firm in December nineteen seventy-three at the age of 64 years.

Thus ends my work history, which has been thrown together in one piece. It would be well, however, to turn backward and consider the family side of our life and to add some to our genealogy picture. We will consider the family history side first. We had returned to Duluth in nineteen forty-six, and the housing picture was bleak. Practically no new homes had been constructed during the war. Viola, Pauline, and I located a small bungalow to rent, opposite the school on Park Point, the strand of soil and sand sticking out in Lake Superior, connected to the mainland by the Aerial Bridge. Viola was pregnant with Sandra, and we had hoped to find housing before her birth, but she beat our house-hunting efforts by two days. We were happy to get moved into our first home even though it was only a tiny one. It would provide us with a base for living while we looked for a place to purchase or to build. So now we were a family of four. Pauline was happy when she could go out and play in the snow, bundled up to her eyes in heavy clothing. Sandra was a big baby. She radiated health and always seemed to be content.

Uncle Fred visited us once while we lived on Park Point, shortly before he moved back to Sweden. It was the last time we would see him. Shortly after returning to Sweden, he married his cousin, Anna, at the age of seventy-two, and lived in retirement in Ljungby.

The last of his generation and of the greatest age, he passed away in nineteen seventy-six, at the age of ninety-five.

one winter day in nineteen forty-six, I returned to the office in the Duluth Christie Building to find my father Charlie waiting for me. We caught a Park Point bus and rode to the cottage where my family and I lived. We placed Sandra in her grandfather's arms. He seemed so pleased to see her and of course Pauline. We didn't know it at the time, but it would be the last time we would see him alive. I rode the bus with him to Sears Roebuck where the milk truck driver was to pick him up for his ride back to Meadowlands.

Then it was Christmas. We were still unable to find a car for sale. It would have been fun to have spent the holiday out at the farm. Failing that, I wrote Mother and Father that Pauline and I would come by train on a weekend in January to visit them. When that Saturday morning arrived, Pauline and I set out by bus to catch the train. Arriving at the Duluth depot we were surprised to see Mr. Berweger, the Meadowlands cheese factory owner, there. He said that he had come to take me to Meadowlands. Since he was a close neighbor of my parents, I thought that he had found out about my proposed visit and had just stopped by after some other business to give us a ride. But then he said, "Perhaps you had better not take Pauline." I answered, "Why, is there something wrong?" He replied, "Your Father passed away early this morning." I was stunned by the news. I knew it was so, but couldn't believe it until I saw Father lying so still in his bed.

The family gathered from California, and from Turtle Lake, Wisconsin, for the funeral.

Mother related how they had had some neighbors in the previous evening for lunch and a visit. The visitors had gone home about eleven in the evening, and the old folks had gone to bed. About three o'clock in the morning, Mother was awakened by some gasping noises that Charlie was making. Just a few seconds, and it was over for him. Mother hurried to him saying, "Charlie, are you leaving me?" She knew, finally that he was dead. She put her bathrobe on, went and turned on all the lights in the house. She even lit a candle in the hall window facing the Hughes' farmhouse nearby. It was a signal seldom used, inviting them to come over for some coffee. But this time they didn't see the light. She did not want to arouse the other neighbors out of their sleep. Taking a hymnal she placed its binding on the table and let go of it. The place where the pages opened up would be the chosen hymn as was done in olden times. The pages opened at "I'm a Pilgrim, I'm a Stranger."

I took over the funeral arrangements. We made or found room for the mourners. The funeral proceeded smoothly, except that shortly before the service Uncle Fred began jumping up and down and crying as though he had lost all control.

When we were about to leave for the church, I asked him whether or not he ought to stay home and avoid grieving so much. He quickly assured me that he would be all right, and he was. It seemed he needed someone to bridle him a little and keep him in control. The chosen hymn was sung by Andrew Anderson, and the funeral sermon preached for this unpretentious Swedish immigrant, the first Mayor of the town. Then out at the cemetery his remains were lowered into the frozen January earth.

In the spring of 1947 I purchased a home at 219 Mulberry Street in Duluth Heights. It was a two story building with a living room, dining room, and kitchen down stairs, and three bedrooms upstairs. We had lots of living space. There were only a few other homes nearby. Outside, there were groves of trees, open fields, and brushland. We were in fact living in the country, though Lowell Grade School was only four blocks down hill, by the Miller Trunk Range Highway. On my birthday, December first, of nineteen forty-seven, Viola gave us the present of our son, Joel. He was our only boy and with his birth, our family was complete. How fast the years went by. Soon the children were all in school. We lived close enough so that they could walk to and from classes.

One day when Joel was trudging up the hill homeward, a half-grown cat stood, in the road. Suddenly a dog charged after the cat, and not knowing what else to do, the cat ran to Joel and climbed to the top of his snowsuit. Joel came walking home with the cat sitting on his head. We returned the cat to its owner, but soon it was back with us. Finally the owner asked us to keep it. So our menagerie began.

One day, while returning from Meadowlands, we spied a small dog in the road ahead. There were no homes for miles around, so we surmised that it was lost. We picked it up and stopped at a few homes, to see if we could reach the owner but to no avail. We sent a note to the area post office with no result. There had been a fatal accident in that vicinity, and it is possible the dog was thrown from the car. He was of the Pekingese breed. He also became part of the family. We removed the collar of ticks that were feeding around his neck, and he was soon ready to play. In winter when the snow was deep, he would climb on the sled to be pulled around by the children, through the snow. We enjoyed "Peeky" for about two years before he was killed by an automobile.

One spring day while coming home from school, the children saw a robin's nest that had been torn from a tree by some boys. Searching the area they found a half-grown robin, alive lying in the grass. They brought it home, and we arranged a nest for it in the back entry of the house. We began a concentrated effort of worm digging to satisfy its voracious appetite, but worms were scarce. Finally we bought sliced bologna lunch meat and cut it into strips for worms; square ones. The robin thrived on them. The children came to me and asked, " What should we name it?" I answered, "Name it Nicodemus, then you can call it Nickie," and so it was called. We would take it outside, and soon it would fly from one to the other of us, lighting on an arm or a shoulder. It would come to our call. We came home from a ride once, and it was gone. I went outside and called "Nickie," and it answered from a tree a half block away. Then it flew closer and began searching the garden for worms. Later that summer, while the pin cherries were still green by the driveway, some of them had been stripped off by little hands and scattered about. Little Nickie tried to eat some and was choked. Of course, there was a funeral, and he was laid to rest in a little paper coffin, behind the garage.

Then there was the year of the bears. Frost had ruined the berry crop back in the forests, and the bears, with a sharp nose for garbage, headed for town. Pauline was on the swing, moving gently back and forth, when she spied one coming. Quick as a wink she headed for the house. As soon as the bear spied Pauline, he took off for the woods.

The bears would return, mostly at night, to spill out the contents of our garbage cans in search of food. One evening, as we sat in the kitchen eating our dinner, we looked out of the window and saw a bear, also eating his dinner of apples from our tree on the back lot. The bears never bothered us, and we made no attempt to get rid of them, but we tried to be extra careful.

Then the children wanted a dog again, and I wanted one for bird hunting. It seemed that the thing to do was to get a Weimaraner for Christmas. I was economizing, and the females were much cheaper, so I purchased one for the Christmas present. We planned to keep it in the basement until spring. A short time previously, Viola's parents had decided to sell their home near Grand Marais, and they had written to us to go there and to take out any furniture that we wanted before it was sold. We hauled a truckload of it home and had stored the overstuffed pieces in the basement. The Weimaraner "Susie" went to work on that furniture and by spring had chewed it to bits. But Susie was a smart dog, and I decided to teach her to retrieve. For a while the training progressed pretty well, but eventually everyone was throwing things for her to retrieve, and she lost interest. She would be a hunting companion and that was all. It was decided to have her bred to a pure-bred Weimaraner to raise some pups for sale and to raise a good male dog for hunting. The following spring she gave birth to eight pups. It was to be the children's project, and we sold four, but when school time arrived in the fall there were still four half-grown hounds left. When I walked into the driveway at night, all four of them would come rushing down the path to meet me, each one asking to be petted. I felt like Dagwood, arriving home. Susie's feet had been run over by neighborhood bicycles, and she began to chase and bite the riders, so she was sold. Three of the pups were also marketed, and we kept one we called, "Mogul." But that winter he contracted English Hard Pad and had to be put to sleep. So except for our cat, the menagerie was no more. Let it suffice to say that the children enjoyed their pets immensely.

We enjoyed them too, but mostly, we enjoyed our children. With their smiles and laughter, their daily comings and goings, their play and accomplishments, and the unfolding of their personalities gave us the best years of our lives. Our home was a good place in which to live. Our doings were much the same as those that take place in any household. The setting was idyllic for young people to grow. To describe it all would be pointless except to say that there was a good quality, a friendly rapport between us, beside the love we had for one another. So, we were thankful for that time which went by all too quickly, but which we will never forget.

We transferred with the Western Electric Company to Oklahoma City in April of nineteen fifty-nine. The children finished grade and high school at the Putnum City Central High School, then went on to various colleges to complete their education. I will leave it to them to carry on with their story, for the enlightenment of future generations.

Left alone on the farm in nineteen forty-seven, Mother Lydia found the loneliness unbearable. Father had always taken care of their business and shopping needs, and she had seldom ventured from the farm. Now, with all of the farm animals sold, she had little to do but remember and look out of her kitchen window to see if someone might be coming for a visit. A few friends did come, but it was not enough to keep her occupied. When summer came, Lillian whisked her off to California. She returned the following summer for another try at living alone. Once again it didn't work out. Back in California she found work in a children's home. In the kitchen again with people around, her spirits rose, and happiness reentered her life. She remained at the home for about three years. The rest of her life was spent living with Margie and Lillian, alternating between California, Florida, and for a time in Poplar, Montana. Once again there was frequent company to entertain, and her daughters allowed her free rein in the kitchen which is what she loved most. At about the age of eighty-eight her superb physique and her mind began to deteriorate. The downhill period lasted for two years and four months. She passed away at the age of ninety years and four months. Margie brought her home on the airplane in June of nineteen seventy. It was lilac time in Meadowlands, the time of year she loved best. Twenty-six years previous, while standing beside her husband Charlie's grave, she had said, "I'll soon be with you Charley." Little did she know how long it would be. Her sons and daughters gathered once again for the funeral, with the exception of Axel, who had been killed in an automobile accident several years before. Those of us remaining had but a short while to visit before returning to our homes far away. There are now no relatives living in Meadowlands. Evidence of the Palmers' thirty-six years of life there can be found only on monuments and headstones in the town cemetery.

During the War years Margie worked as a secretary for an insurance company in San Diego. She met Larry Paulson in nineteen forty-three, and they were married in nineteen forty-four while he was yet in the Marines. He embarked in the bankers profession, beginning at a bank in Coronado. Their first child, Pamela was born in nineteen forty-six. They moved to Highland Park, Arcadia, and last of all in California, to Monrovia. Bruce was born in nineteen forty-nine in the Alhambra Hospital. In nineteen fifty-six they moved out of California, first to Kewanee, Illinois, then East Gary, and finally to Pompano Beach, Florida, where Larry worked at the First National Bank until he retired in nineteen seventy-three.

Six years after mother Lydia'.s funeral in Meadowlands, the remaining Palmers gathered there again to lay our oldest sister, Lillian to rest beside her parents. It is likely that she will be the last of the family to be buried there. Andrew Anderson, who, twenty-nine years before, had sung the chosen hymn for Father, sang once more, for Lillian. Many old friends arrived to attend the graveside service. One of them, Cary Branson, remarked that a young resident had recently asked, "Who are the Palmers?"

It was startling to be reminded that though we had lived in the community for thirty-six years, most of the residents did not know us. But then we had been living elsewhere for twenty-eight years.

On August twenty-first and twenty-second of nineteen seventy-six, a high school reunion was held at the Meadowlands High School for classes that had graduated in the years of nineteen twenty-six through nineteen thirty-one. We gathered in the old high school gymnasium. It appeared that those of us who had come the farthest arrived in the gym first.

Each time a pair of new arrivals entered and came down the stairs, we would stare at them muttering, "Now who is that?" It turned out that we had all changed so much that many of us didn't know each other. Finally, everyone got their name tags on, and we were spared the embarrassment of guessing who we were talking to.

The fine program and the dinner prepared for us left little time for reminiscing. But for a short time we were together again, and it was well worth the time and travel. Much of the lusty bustle is gone from the village of Meadowlands. Many of the residents are old and retired. Farming, the mainstay of living in the early years, had largely come to a halt. About ninety percent of those living on farms rent their hay stumpage to a contractor. The active residents earn their livelihood working in the Iron Range mines, the iron pelletizing plants, or in Duluth, planting few crops on their farmland.

The town might now be described as a bedroom community from which people commute to their work. It has become an old village, lying peacefully in the sun and the snow, between the Whiteface and St. Louis rivers. Nearly all of the early settlers are gone, many of them gathered to rest in the cemetery east of town. They have dreamed their dreams and lived their time. Thinking back over the early years, Lydia once said, "We didn't know it then, but those were the best years of our lives."